Python

Programming

This Book Includes:

Python for Data Analysis

and Science with Big Data

Analysis, Statistics and

Machine Learning.

sources. Please consult a licensed professional before attempting any techniques outlined in this book.

By reading this document, the reader agrees that under no circumstances is the author responsible for any losses, direct or indirect, which are incurred as a result of the use of information contained within this document, including, but not limited to, — errors, omissions, or inaccuracies.

Table of Contents

Python for Data Analysis

A Complete Guide for Beginners, Including Python Statistics and Big Data Analysis

Introduction

Congratulations on purchasing *Python for Data Analysis,* and thank you for doing so.

The following chapters will discuss all of the things that we need to know when it is time to work on our own data analysis for the first time. Many companies have heard about data analysis and are curious to know how this works and what they are able to do with it. However, many are not sure the right steps to take in order to see the best results. This guidebook is not only going to walk you through completing your own data analysis but will ensure that you are set and able to do it all with the Python coding language as well.

This guidebook is going to look at some of the basics that you need to do in order to start with your own data analysis. This is going to ensure that you are set to start this process on your own and that you will see some of the results of better decision making, cutting down waste, beating out the competition, and reaching your customers better than ever before.

To start with this process, we spent a bit of time learning more about the data analysis and what this is all about. There are a number of steps that we need to know about in order to get started with this process, and we will talk about the basics of data analysis, some of the benefits of working with this process, and the steps or the lifecycle that works with our data analysis as well.

Once we have some time to look through data analysis and how it works, it is time for us to move into the Python language. There are a number of different coding languages that we are able to use along with our data analysis, but the Python language has some of the best libraries and the best tools to help to get this done. In addition, a language is simple and easy to use. This guidebook will take some time to discuss why the Python language is such a good choice to use when it comes to doing this data analysis and how you can get it all started.

From there, we need to spend some time on a few of the best libraries that will work for our data analysis and are connected to the Python language as well. We will start with the NumPy library, which is designed to work for most of the other libraries as well since they rely on the arrays that are found in this library. We can then move on to the Matplotlib library, the Pandas library, and some of the reasons why you would want to work with the IPython environment rather than the traditional option that is out there.

To end this guidebook, we have a few more parts that we need to spend some time on as well. We are going to look at the basics of data visualizations and why we would want to use these, some of the best tools that work so well with the Python language and some of the industries and practical applications that come with using the Python data analysis for your own business as well.

There are a ton of benefits that show up when we talk about the Python data analysis and any industry, and any business will be able to benefit when they choose to use this for their own needs as well. When you are ready to learn some more about the Python language and how it can work to improve your data analytic skills to help your business, make sure to check out this guidebook to help you get started.

Chapter 1: Introduction of Python and Python's History

There are many different coding languages out there that we are able to work with. Learning how these work and what they can help us to create is such a wonderful thing in the projects that we can create. However, we need to make sure that we are learning the right coding language for our needs.

When it comes to working with data analysis and all of the different parts that come with that process, the Python language is one of the best. Sure, there are other options out there that we can choose from, but none will provide us with the ease of use, the power, the different libraries and extensions, and more, that will truly make our data analysis shine and provide us with the answers and results that we need.

With that in mind, it is time for us to take a closer look at the Python language and learn a bit more about it. We need to learn the history of the Python language and why it is one of the best out there for us to learn from. In addition, we need to look at some of the ways that we are able to use the Python language in order to get the full use out of it as well. Let us dive in and see how this can work!

The History of Python

Python is a very popular programming language that is high-level and general-purpose. It was designed in 1991 by Guido van Rossum and then developed by Python Software Foundation. It was developed in the beginning with an emphasis on having codes that were readable to all, and the syntax was made to help programmers find better ways to express the concepts that they wanted in fewer lines of code.

During the late 1980s, history was about to be written brand new. It was during this time when some of the work on the modern Python language first began. Soon after this time, Guido van Rossum began doing some of the application based work in 1989 at the Centrum Wiskunde and Informatica, which was found in the Netherlands.

Working on the Python language was just a hobby project to get started because van Rossum was just looking for something that could capture his interest during the Christmas break. The programming language, which Python is known to have succeeded, is the ABC Programming language.

ABC was something that van Rossum had worked to create earlier on in his own career, but he had seen that there were a few issues with the features and more of this language. After some time, he decided that he needed to go through and make some changes to improve it, which led him to take the syntax of the ABC language, and some of the good features that were still found in it, and make it into something new.

The inspiration that is found with the name of this language was from Monty Python's Flying Circus since van Rossum was a big fan of this and he wanted to come up with a name that was unique, short, and maybe even a bit mysterious for the invention he was working with on Python. Van Rossum continued to work as the leader on this language until July of 2018, but he was considered a benevolent dictator who allowed other developers to work on the language with many free reigns to give us the language that we know and live today.

The official Python language was released in 1991. When this release happened, it used a lot fewer codes in order to express the concepts of coding when compared with other languages like C++, C, and Java. The design philosophy that came with this was good compared to the others.

For the most part, the main objective that we can see with the Python language is that it was to provide readable code and a lot of productivity that was advanced for the developer.

Why Use Python?

The neat thing about working with Python is that it has something for everyone to enjoy along the way. There are tons of benefits that come with it, and it really does not matter if you have worked with programming in the past or not. You will still find something to love about Python, and it is something that is easy to work with for all levels of programming. Some of the different reasons why you may want to work with the Python language overall include:

1. **It has some code that is maintainable and readable.**

While you are writing out some of the applications for the software, you will need to focus on the quality of source code in order to simplify some of the updates and the maintenance. The syntax rules of Python are going to allow you a way to express the concepts without having to write out any additional codes. At the same time, Python, unlike some of the other coding languages out there, is going to emphasize the idea of the readability of the code and can allow us to work with keywords in English instead of working with different types of punctuations for that work.

Because of this, you can get a lot more done with Python. It is possible to work with Python in order to build up some custom applications, without us having to write additional code. The readable and clean code base is going to make it easier to maintain and then update the software without having to go through and add in more time and effort to the process.

2. Comes with many programming paradigms.

Another benefit that we will see is the multiple programming paradigms. Like some of the other coding languages that we can find, Python is going to support more than one programming paradigm inside of it. This is going to be a language that can support structured and oriented programming to the fullest. In addition, a language will feature some support for various concepts when it comes to functional and aspect-oriented programming.

Along with all of this, the Python language is going to feature a kind of system that is dynamically typed and some automatic management of the memory. The programming paradigms and language features will help us to work with Python to develop complex and large software applications when we would like.

3. Compatible with most major systems and platforms.

Right now, Python is going to be able to support many different operating systems. It is even possible to work with interpreting to run the code on some of the specific tools and platforms that we want to use. In addition, since this is known as a language that is interpreted, it is going to allow us to go through and run the exact same code on many different platforms, without the need of doing any recompilation.

Because of this, you are not required to recompile the code when you are done altering it. You can go through and run the application code that you modified without recompiling and checking the impact of the changes that happened to that code right away. The feature makes it a lot easier to go through and make some changes to the code without having to worry about the development time along the way.

4. A very robust standard library.

The standard library that works with Python is robust and has many different parts that go with it. The standard library is a good one to provide us with all of the modules that we need to handle. Each module is further going to enable us to add some of the functionality to the Python application without needing to write out the additional code.

For example, if you are using Python to help write out a new web application, it is possible to use some specific modules to help with the web services, perform operations on strings, manage the interface of the operating system, or work with some of the internet protocols. You are even able to go through and gather some of the information on the other modules through the documentation of the Python Standard Library.

5. Can simplify some of the work that you are doing.

Python is seen as a programming language that is general purpose in nature. This means that you are able to use this language for all of the different processes and programs that you want to, from web applications to developing things like desktop applications as needed. We can even take it further and use this language to help develop complex scientific and numeric applications.

Python was designed with a lot of features that are there to facilitate the data analysis and visualizations that we will talk about in this guidebook. In addition, you can take advantage of these features in Python in order to create some custom big data solutions without having to put in the extra effort or time.

Along the same lines, the libraries for data visualizations and APIs that are provided by Python are going to help us to visualize and present the data in a more appealing and effective manner. Many developers of Python will use this to help them with tasks of natural language processing and artificial intelligence.

As we can see, there are a number of benefits that we are able to enjoy when it comes to using the Python language, and this is just the beginning. As we go through and learn more about how to work in this language and what it is able to do for us. We are able to see more and more of the benefits at the same time, and it will not take long working with your own data analysis to understand exactly how great this can be for our needs.

Chapter 2: Data Analysis

Now that we have a bit of an understanding of the Python language and all that it entails, it is time for us to look at the main event of data analysis. Learning how to work with the Python language is great, but real-world applications are some of the best ways to learn a language and make it worth our time a bit more. Python works great with data analysis, so let us look at what data analysis is all about and how we can use it for some of our own needs.

To start, data analysis is going to be the process of cleaning, inspecting, transforming, and modeling our data with the objective of finding some of the most useful information in it, coming to some sound conclusions, and then supporting the decision making the process of a company. This sounds like a lot for one process to handle, but when we use the right algorithms (supplied to us and run by Python). It is definitely possible.

There are going to be a lot of different approaches and facets that come with our data analysis, and when we put it all together, we will be able to choose from a wide number of techniques to get it done. Often it depends on which method we like the most and what information we are hoping to get out of the process as well. If our goals are to learn about our customers and how they behave, the data analysis we will complete will be different from if we are trying to learn more about the competition in our industry, or even different from when we want to use it to make good business decisions.

When we use data analysis in statistics, we are able to divide it up quite a bit. We can divide this up into things like exploratory data analysis, descriptive statistics, and confirmatory data analysis. All of these are going to be important when it comes to our data analysis and can move us forward to finding all of the insights and more, inside of the work that we do.

Another important aspect that we have to pay attention to in our data analysis is the fact that data has to be cleaned. Data cleaning is going to be a long process, but it allows us to correct all of the outliers that could mess with our results and helps us to get rid of the other information that is unwanted and incorrect in the process. There are a number of these cleaning processes on the data, and it depends on the kind of data that we would like to clean. If you are working with things like quantitative data, then we can work with outlier detection to help ensure that the anomalies in our data are taken care of. Even things like spellcheckers can be useful in case we are working with textual data and need to deal with some of the words that have been mistyped.

In some cases, our data analysis is going to turn into a form of business intelligence. This is when the data analysis that we use is going to run heavily on aggregation, disaggregation, dicing and slicing, and even focusing on some of the information that is the most important to our business. This is just one of the forms that we are able to use, though. We can move into the world of predictive analytics as well because this helps us to apply the statistical and the structural models that we have for some predictive forecasting when necessary. Alternatively, there is the text analytics available, which is going to be the application of the statistical, structural, and linguistic models to help us extract and classify the information that is found in the text.

While all of these forms handle data in a slightly different manner, and we are going to use them in a manner that is different from one another, they are all important, and we need to spend time on them. In addition, all of them, even though they may seem to be completely different from one another, are going to be types of data analysis!

Many businesses want to jump on board with this kind of analysis. They have heard about the great results that many other companies have experienced with this, and they want to be able to do it as well. This makes it the perfect choice for them to at least look into and you will find with a bit of research that almost any industry is able to benefit when they start to complete their own data analysis.

This is already such a big part of our world. Companies in all of the different industries are finding that this is the way of the future. It helps them to make better products that customers want, helps them to make better decisions, helps them to beat out the competition, and even helps them to reach their customers in new and innovative manners. Because of all the benefits that come with the data analysis, it is no wonder that so many businesses are interested in working with the data analysis and making sure that they can use it in the proper manner.

What is Data Analysis?

When it comes to working with data analysis, there are going to be a few methods that you are able to work with. These phases will ensure that you can handle the data in the proper manner and that it will work the way that we want it to. These are going to include some of the initial phases of cleaning our data, working with whether the data is high enough quality, quality measurement analysis, and then we enter into the main data analysis.

All of these steps are going to be important to the work that we want to do with data analysis. Without all of them, even though some may seem to have nothing to do with data analysis in the first place, our analysis is not going to be very accurate or good. Since companies are often going to rely on these analyses for important decisions, having accurate and high-quality data is going to be important.

The first step that we need to focus on here is data cleaning. This is the first process, and while it may not be as much fun as we see with the algorithms and more that come with data analysis, they are still important. This is the part of the process where we match up records, check for multiples and duplicates in the data, and get rid of anything that is false or does not match up with what we are looking for at this time.

When that part is done with the part of cleaning our data, it is time for us to go through and do a bit of quality assurance here. We want to make sure that the data we work with is going to work for any algorithm that we would like to focus our time and attention on. Using things like frequency counts and descriptive statistics can help us out with this.

It is never a good idea to go through and analyze data that does not meet some of your own personal standards. You want to make sure that it will match up with what you want to do with some of your work on the analysis, that it is accurate, and it will get the job done for you, as well.

When the quality analysis part is done, it is time to make sure that the measurement tools that we use here are going to be higher in quality as well. If you are not using the same measurements on each part of this, then your results will be skewed in the process. If you are using the right ones, though, you will find that this gives you some options that are more accurate and can help you really rely on the data analysis.

Once the whole process of making sure you clean the data, and we have done the quality analysis and the measurement, it is time to dive into the analysis that we want to use. There are a ton of different analysis that we can do on the information, and it often will depend on what your goals are in this whole process. We can go through and do some graphical techniques that include scattering plots. We can work with some frequency counts to see what percentages and numbers are present. We can do some continuous variables or even the computation of new variables.

There are tons of algorithms that are present when we work on this, and it will again depend on your goals. Some are better for helping you to see the best decision to make out of several options, such as the decision tree and random forest. Others are going to be better for helping us to sort through our information and see what patterns are there, such as the clustering algorithms. Having a good idea of what you are looking for out of the data and what you hope to gain from it can make a world of difference.

The Main Data Analysis

Now it is time for us to go through and work with what is known as the main data analysis. There are many parts that come with this as well, and we have to remember that this is a big process. It will take some time and is not always as easy and straightforward as we would hope in the beginning. During this part, after we have had a chance to go through and clean the data and get it organized, including cleaning it off and some of the work that we did before, it is time to enter into the main data analysis in order to get some things done in the manner that we want.

There are a few methods that we need to use to make this work. For example, the confirmatory and the exploratory approaches will help us out. These are not going to allow us to have a clear hypothesis stated before we analyze the data. This ensures that we are not going to be tempted to bring in our ideas to the mix. We will go through the information and see what is there, and I hope that be able to learn something from it in the process.

Then we are able to check on some of the stability that shows up in the results. The stability of the results using cross-validation, statistical methods, and sensitivity analysis is going to help. We want to make sure that the results we are able to get are accurate and will be able to repeat themselves. If we run through it a few times and end up with a few different answers, how are we supposed to know which result is the right one for us? This takes some time and dedication to be done but can be the right method to help us out.

We can then work with a few different methods of statistics to help us pick out the algorithm that we want to work with and to make sure that we can see what is going on with everything. Some of the statistical methods that we are able to utilize here will include:

1. The general linear model: There are a number of models of statistics that are going to work with the general linear model in order to get things done. This is going to help us to work with some of the dependent variables that are there, and we can even work with what is known as a multiple linear regression if there are several of these dependent variables as well.

2. Generalized linear model: This is similar to the other option that we talked about, but it is often considered as more of a generalization or the extension of that model. It

is used to help with some of the discrete dependent variables that are out there.

3. Item response theory. The models that are used for this one are going to spend time assessing one latent variable from some of the other binary measured variables that are out there.

In addition to this, there are tons of different approaches that you can use to analyze your data. They can all be fun, and in some cases, you will be able to utilize more than one of these at a time. It all depends on what you want to do with the data. A few of the options that are available to try out include:

1. A cross-cultural analysis to see if the same results are going to happen between different countries or different cultures.

2. Content analysis

3. The grounded theory analysis

4. The discourse analysis

5. The narrative analysis

6. The hermeneutic analysis

7. The ethnographic analysis.

Keep in mind that when we are doing some of the data analysis work that we want to accomplish, a lot of it is going to have nothing to do with the actual analysis that we want to use. There will be a good deal of time spent on understanding the data at hand and cleaning it off. In addition, we even need to take care in picking out the right algorithm that we want to use.

That does not mean that the analysis is not important. However, for the analysis to truly work, we need to make sure that all of those other parts are in place and working well too. This ensures that we have high-quality data that can train our machine learning algorithms well and provide us with some of the results that we want in the process. When we take our time and really do the previous steps in the proper manner, we know with certainty that the results and insights that we get from the actual data analysis will be accurate and can work for our needs as well.

Chapter 3: Why Choose Python for Data Analysis?

We spent the first two chapters take a look at two very important topics. We talked about the Python language and some of its history, along with some of the reasons that so many people love to work with Python for their coding needs. Then we moved on to a discussion about data analysis and how this can be a good way for companies to take in many data and learn from it along the way. These are two very important topics that we can take our time on, but now it is time for us to figure out how both of them go together.

At some point in your data analysis, you will need to create some models or some algorithms that will allow you to sort through that data and find the insights that work the best for you. This is hard to do sometimes, and some challenging codes will come with it. However, as we will discuss in this chapter, the Python language can take all of that and make it as simple to work with as possible.

It is Easy to Read and Simple

We are going to start this off by looking at some of the reasons why Python, in particular, is such a good coding language to choose for our data analysis needs. There are other languages that we can work with, and they do a very good job as well. However, there are some wonderful things about Python that helps to push it above the rest and will ensure that you will get the best results when you work on this process as well.

While those who are in more scientific and engineering backgrounds may feel a bit out of place when they first start to work with the Python language, they will find that over time, the readability and the simplicity that comes with this language is going to make it easy to pick up. In addition, when we add in that it has many dedicated libraries to data analysis and even machine learning, we know that data scientists, no matter what industry or sector they are in, will be able to find some of the packages they need, ones that are tailored to their needs. In addition, for the most part, these libraries and extensions are going to be freely available to download.

Of course, this should not be a huge surprise. Python had many potentials to be expanded out, and since it is general-purpose in nature, it is easy to see why this popularity would bring it out into the field of data analytics. As a kind of a jack of all trades in the coding world, it was not necessarily a language that was suited to work with statistical analysis. However, there are many organizations and more out there to invested in this language and worked to create the extensions and libraries, which made Python the perfect choice to work with.

Because of the simplicity that comes with Python, the fact that anyone can learn how to use it no matter what their background is all about, and the fact that it is going to be easy to extend out to meet all of the capabilities that you want, it is easy to see why this is a language that is thriving in the world of data analysis.

The Libraries are Nice to Work with

As is the case when we look at some of the other popular coding languages, it is going to be some of the libraries that come with Python that will really lead to the success that you can see. In fact, right now, it is believed that in the Python Package Index, there are about 72000 libraries there, and this is a number that is constantly growing.

With this language designed to have a core that is lightweight and stripped down, the standard library has been built up with many tools to handle all of the different programming tasks that are out there. It is seen as a philosophy of "batteries included" that will allow the users of the language to get down in a timely and efficient manner, all of the nuts and bolts of solving problems without having to do a lot of work to find the right function libraries to get it done.

Because Python is free and open-sourced, it is possible for anyone to come in and write their own library package that is able to extend out what Python can do. Moreover, data science has been one of the earliest beneficiaries of this overall. In particular, Pandas has come out of all this, and it is the number one data analysis library to get things done.

Pandas is used for anything that you want to do when it comes to data analysis. It can do it all from importing data from an Excel spreadsheet to processing some of the sets that are necessary for time-series analysis. Pandas have been able to make it so that all of the common tools that are used for data munging are right at your fingertips. This means that things like basic cleanup and some advanced manipulation can be performed when we use the powerful data frames that come with it.

Another thing to consider is that the Pandas library has been built on top of the NumPy library, which is one of the earliest libraries that came with Python for data science. The functions that come with NumPy are going to be exposed in Pandas so that we are able to finish off our advanced numeric analysis in the process.

Now, those are just two of the different libraries that we can focus on when we go through this process. If you want to know about a few more of the options, or you need something that is a bit more specialized, you will still be able to find it. Some of the other choices that a programmer can make when they work with data analysis and the Python language include:

1. **SciPy:** This is going to be similar to NumPy, but it focuses more on the sciences that we need. It is also good at providing us with some tools and techniques so that we can analyze the scientific data to meet our needs.

2. **Statsmodels:** This library is going to focus more on some of the tools that are used for statistical analysis.

3. **Scikit-Learn and PyBrain:** These two libraries are going to be focused more on machine learning. They are good ones to use when you need some modules for building neural networks and for doing some data preprocessing.

4. **SymPy:** This is going to be a good one to use for statistical applications.

5. **PyMC PyLearn2, Shogun:** This is a good one to help with some of the work that we want to do within machine learning.

6. **Matplotlib, Seaborn, and Plotly:** As we will discuss as we go through this guidebook, the visuals that come with your analysis are going to be important. The three libraries that we have above are going to be good ones to help you take your data and then turn it into a visual to help you see what insights and patterns are there a little bit better.

Remember that these are just a few of the libraries that you can work within data analysis. There are libraries, and most of them are free to use, which are available for pretty much anything you want to do in the Python and data analysis world. Moreover, this is one of the benefits of working with Python here. It allows us to come out and work with any library and extension that we want. In addition, if there happens not to be an available library to work with, then there is the option, since Python is open-sourced, for us to go out there and make one of our own to meet this need.

The Large Community

In addition, the final big reason of why we would want to choose to work with the Python coding language to help with our data analysis is that there is a large community, which means there is always someone who is there to help us out when we need it. There is a broad and diverse base of millions of Python coding users who are there and more than happy to offer suggestions or advice when you are stuck on something. If you are struggling with something, then it is highly likely that someone else in this community has been stuck there in the past. In addition, they can provide you with some tips and tricks in order to handle that and get out of the problem.

While open-source communities will have policies that allow for open discussion, there are some for other languages that are not as user-friendly, and they may not open up their arms for beginners as well as you would like. This can be intimidating and can easily turn people off from these other languages. When you want to learn something new and how to actually accomplish some of your codings, the last thing that you want to worry about is whether the community is going to be open and inviting to some of your questions, or if they will get mad and try to chase you off.

On the other hand, we can look at the Python community. This is going to be a big exception to some of those other communities. Both the local meetup groups and online will provide you with a ton of Python experts who are able and willing to help you go through and figure out some of the different intricacies that come with learning a new language. Even though Python is an easier language to learn than some of the other ones, there are still times when you are going to need some help. This is never truer than when we are working with data analysis.

The people who work with Python and who are in these communities are there and willing to help. They remember that they chose this language because it was simple, and they were scared of trying to make it work. Therefore, they are usually more willing to help others who are in the same kind of situation.

In addition, since Python is growing and becoming ever so prevalent in the community of data science, there are going to be a ton of resources that you can use. These resources are going even to be specific to working with the Python language in the field of data science. This can help you get the help and the assistance that you need when working on some of your projects along the way.

As we can see here, many benefits come with Python. We talked about a few of them here in this chapter and a few in the first chapter in this guidebook. It is amazing to see how many people can take to the Python language quickly and effectively, and it is one that you will want to try out for your own needs as well. When it comes to working with data analysis, the Python language is the best choice to help you learn and get things done quickly and efficiently.

Chapter 4: Understanding the Data Analytics Process

Now it is time for us to look a bit more into some of the mechanics that are there for a good data analysis. All of these need to be in place to ensure that the data analytics is going to work, that we get the right kind of data, and that we will be able to get all of it to flow together and do well. This is sometimes a difficult process to work with, but you will find that when we combine the parts and make sure that we understand how they work, it is easier to see what we need to do to get this done. With that in mind, let us look at the six main phases that come with data analysis and explore what we can do with each one.

The Discovery Phase

This is a fun phase to work with because it can set the stage for the rest of the project that we need to work on. This part is all about figuring out what kind of data we need, what our goals are, and what we would actually like to figure out later on after the whole analysis is done. We do not want to take this part lightly, and it usually is not a good idea to just go and gather up a bunch of data without first figuring out what we need and what we want to do.

We want to start out with a good idea of what the business wants to accomplish when they do this analysis. Do they want to figure out more about their customer base? Do they want to learn if there is a new niche, they can go into? Do they want to learn more about their competition and how they can utilize that information to get ahead? There are many reasons that companies want to use the data analysis, but if you do not have a plan in place ahead of time, then it is going to be a mess. You will waste time gathering up information, with no plan at all.

When this is done, it is time for us to figure out which methods we will use for gathering up the data. Data analysis is going to be useless if we are not able to go through and discover the data that we want to use in our algorithms. The good news is that there are tons of places with data in our modern world, and we just need to do some research and figure out which ones are going to provide us with the data that we need.

We can choose to spend some time on social media and see what people are saying to us or how they are interacting with us. We can send out surveys and do focus groups to learn a bit. We can do research online and on some websites to figure out what is going on there. We can look to our own websites and see what customers are buying and some of the demographics that match up there as well.

There is no limit to the amount of information that we can gather, but we want to ensure that we are gathering up the right kind of information in the process. Just because you have many data at your disposal does not mean that you are going to use it well, or that it is even relevant to what you are trying to be done. Take your time when it comes to gathering up that data and figure out what is important and what is not.

The Data Preparation Phase

Once you have had some time to prepare for the information that you want, and to figure out what questions you would like to see solved in the process, it is time for us to go through and work with the phase of data preparation. At this point, we have a bunch of data from a bunch of different places and sources. This is a great thing. However, you will not have to search through the data very long to figure out that, it is a mess, and that there is some work for you to do to get it ready.

If you try to push your data through the chosen algorithm in its current state, you are not going to get accurate information and results. The algorithm will be confused at what you are trying to do along the way. There will be missing values, incomplete entries, duplicates, outliers that can throw off the average, and more. Despite the extra work that is going to happen here, your algorithms require that the data you want to be interpreted is organized and prepared in the proper manner.

There are a few things that we need to focus on in order to make this happen. First, we need to deal with outliers. These are going to be the points that are way far from the average and were just some once in a lifetime kind of things. If the majority of your customers are between the ages of 18 to 25, but you have a couple of customers who are 75, the older group can probably be ignored.

Those were likely individuals purchasing stuff for someone in the younger group. However, if you add them into the mix and put them through the algorithm, it is going to skew your results. You may, if you leave these outliers in there, start to think your age demographics are individuals 30 to 35 because the older group messed with things a bit and took the average too high.

Now, this does not mean that we get rid of the outliers all of the time. Many times it does, but there are some situations where the outliers are going to tell us a lot of information in the process. If there are a decent number of outliers that fall in the same spot, this could be a goldmine, telling you of a new product or a new demographic that you could possibly reach. Maybe the average age of your customer is 18 to 25, but then you look and see there is a concentration of outliers in the 30 to 35 range. This may be something that you need to explore in more detail and then capitalize on.

In addition to working with the outliers, we need to spend some time looking at the duplicate values. Sometimes especially since we are gathering data from many different sources, we are going to end up with some information that is duplicated. This is not a big deal if it is just a few sources. However, when we have many duplicates, it is going to mess with the results that you get. It is often best to reduce and even eliminate the duplicates to get the best results.

In addition, the final thing that we need to focus on when it comes to our data preparation is to make sure that the missing values are taken care of. If you have a few missing values, then you can probably erase that part of the data and be fine. However, many times, filling it in with the mean or the average of the other columns with it can be a good way to still use that information without getting error messages from your algorithm.

Planning Out the Model Phase

Now it is time for us to move on to some model planning. This is where you and your team are going to start creating the model or the algorithms that you want to use in order to move this process along and ensure that it is going to work the way that you want. Based on the work that you did in the other two steps, the model that you choose to use is going to vary, and this is the stage where we figure out the best steps to take.

During this part, the team is going to spend some time determining which workflow, techniques, and methods are going to be needed to help us later when we build up our model. We figure out how we can best use the data that we have been collecting all this time, and work from there. The team will also need to explore some of the data they have to learn more about the relationship that is there between the variables, and then they can select the variables that are the most important here.

The reason that we are going to do this is that it helps us to figure out the models that are the most suitable to work with. When we know more about the variables, and we can find the pattern of the ones that are the most important to our needs, the model will lend itself to us pretty well. This can save us a lot of time and effort and can make sure that we do not have to work on a bunch of different models in the hopes that we will get the right one.

The Model Building Phase

The fourth phase that we are able to spend our time on is model building. This is going to be where we get to work figuring out how to make a model that can learn from the input it gets and will be able to sort through some of the data that we have as well. It is a great phase to work with and can be seen as some of the most fun as well.

In this phase, your team is going to take time developing the sets of data that they want to use for testing, training, and for various production purposes for their algorithms as well. In addition, in this phase, the team builds and then executes the models based on some of the work that has been done in the previous phase as well.

In addition, the team here is going to take the time to consider whether the tools that it already has will be enough to run the models. Sometimes they have the right tools and more to get it all done and other times they will need to go through and add in a more robust environment for executing their models and some of the workflows that they want to accomplish.

The Communication Phase

Once you have had a chance to work on building your model and pushing the chosen data through it, it is time for us to look at some of the key insights and patterns that are there, and communicate them to others around us. This data analysis was likely done for some reason, usually to help a company in the process, and the team who did this work must be able to help communicate this to the right people.

Sometimes, this is going to be a challenge. The individuals in the company who order this analysis may recognize the importance of doing it and want to get the results. However, they may not understand all of the technical terms like a data analyst can. It is up to you and your team to communicate the results clearly and concisely to the audience.

In this phase, the team, along with some of the major stakeholders in the company, are going to determine whether the results of the project are going to be a success or a failure based on some of the criteria that were set out in the first phase we talked about before. The team needs to be able to identify some of the key findings, quantify the business value of this, and then go through and develop a narrative to help convey and summarize the findings so everyone can understand and use them.

There are a number of methods that can be used to help communicate the results. You can use visuals to help show it, along with some spreadsheets and reports. Think about your audience before you get started on this one to ensure that you are presenting the data in a manner that the other party will be able to use and understand.

Operationalize

The final phase that we are going to look at here is to operationalize. This is where the team is going to take all of the work that we were able to handle and look over in the other five steps, and then deliver it to those who need it. This includes the technical documents, codes, briefings, and all of the final reports as well.

In addition, depending on the results of this, and what the suggestions and insights are all about, the company may decide to take this information and run a kind of pilot project. This allows them to implement some of the models and the other insights into a production environment, and see how it is going to work. If things go well, the company may decide that it is time to take this further and try it out in other parts of the company, and their business, as well.

Each of these stages of data analytics is important. This will ensure that we are able to go through, organize things, and get it ready to handle some of the data using our algorithms along the way. If this process is done well, and the right care and attention are given to it all, you will find that it is easier for us to learn those insights and predictions, and we can utilize that to help us become more successful in the long-term.

Chapter 5: NumPy Package Installation

Earlier, we took some time to look at the different libraries that come with the Python language, and the ones that will work the best with data analysis. With that in mind, it is time for us to start working with some of the steps to installing the most basic, but also important, the library is known as NumPy.

We are going to install this on all three of the major operating systems to make it easier, and we will use the pip, which is the package installer for Python. This will make it easier to get things done and will ensure that the NumPy library is going to work on any computer that you would like. We can then talk about some of the basics of working with NumPy later on, so we see why this library is such an imprint one to work with.

Installing NumPy on a Mac OS

The first operating system that we will look at is how to install the NumPy on our Mac computers. We can do this with several different Python versions, and the steps are similar to one another to make things easier. To start, we need to open up the terminal on your computer. In addition, you get that open, type in python to get the prompt for this language to open for you. When you get to this part, follow the steps below to help get it going:

1. We want to press on Command and then the Space Bar. This will help us to open up the spotlight search. Type in the word "Terminal" before pressing on entering.

2. This should bring up the terminal that we want to use. We can then use the command of pip in order to install the NumPy package. This requires the coding of "pip install numpy" to get going.

3. Once you have gotten a successful install, you can type in python to this again to get that python prompt. You should check to see which version of python is displayed there. You can then choose to use your command of import in order to include the package of NumPy and use it in any codes that you would like in the future.

That method works the best with Python 2.7. You can also go through and install the NumPy package on Python 3. This is going to be similar. However, when you are done opening the terminal that we detailed in the first step above, you would use the pip3 command in order to install NumPy. Notice that we are going to work with pip3 rather than pip from before. Otherwise, the steps are going to be the same.

Installing NumPy on a Windows System

It is important to remember that the Python language is not going to be on the Windows operating system by default, so we need to go through and do the installation on our own to use it. You can go to www.python.org and find the version that you want to use. Follow the steps that are there in order to get Python ready to go on your own computer. Once you have been able to get Python installed successfully, you can then open up the command prompt that is on your computer and use pip in order to install the NumPy library.

Installing NumPy on the Ubuntu Operating Systems

Ubuntu and some of the Linux distributions may not be as common and as popular to work with as some of the other options out there, but they can still do many amazing things when it comes to helping us get our work done. It is a good option to use for things like hacking, machine learning, and data analysis, and it is known to work well with the Python language.

You will find that similar to the Mac operating system, Python is going to already be installed on this kind of computer. However, there is a problem because the pip is not going to be installed. If you would like to have the complete package to get this work done, download this from www.python.org, and then get it installed on your operating system using the apt install command to get this done.

In addition, there is an alternative manner to get this done. You can work with the install pip command on ubuntu and then install NumPy. This is often the better of the two ways to do it because it is simple and just needs a few commands. Keep in mind with this one that you have to have the root privileges on your system to help install pip and NumPy, or it will not work.

You can do all of this by opening up the terminal that is found in ubuntu and then install pip with the command of "pip3 using apt". Once you have this pip installed on your computer, you can then go through and install NumPy with the same commands that you used in the other operating systems.

Installing NumPy on Fedora

Another option that we are going to use is known as the Fedora operating system. This one is a bit different than we will see with some of the other options, but it does have a few of the steps that the Ubuntu system from before has. We are going to work with the pip command to help install the NumPy library.

Notice that there is going to be a difference in the command of pip whether you are using it for Python 2.X or Python 3 and higher. This is specifically seen when we are working with the Fedora system. We will need to use pip install numpy to get the older version, but we will want to work with python3 -m pi install numpy for the newer versions.

It is easy to get both the Python language and the NumPy library installed in our computers, and no matter which operating system you decide to work with along the way, it is going to be an easy process to work with and get the library up and running. Once that is done, you can start to use this library directly, or use it as the main source to help some of the other libraries run and get to the arrays, which we will talk about in a bit.

Chapter 6: NumPy Array Operations

Once you have had a chance to go through and install the NumPy array that you want to use, it is time to go through and see what the array can do in this library. This is an important part of working with data analysis because it allows us to get a lot of work done, and many of the other data analysis libraries are going to rely on these arrays. With this in mind, we need to take a closer look at what the NumPy array is all about and what we can do with it.

What are the Arrays in NumPy?

NumPy is able to provide us with a huge set of functionalities over some of the traditional list or array in Python. It is going to be useful when it is time to perform some of the operations that we want on things like the mathematical aggregations, algebraic operations, local operations, and we can even use this to help us slice and dice our chosen array.

Anyone who is working with this library to help with deep learning, machine learning, or data analysis with Python will find that taking the time to learn what NumPy is all about and how we can use this is the first step to the process. There are several things that we need to know about these NumPy arrays in order to get them to work well for our needs, and these include:

1. The Python NumPy array is going to be a very helpful tool when it comes to working with data analysis. It is going to be an efficient multi-dimensional container of values that have the same numeric type.

2. It is going to come in with a powerful wrapper of the n-dimensional arrays in Python, which is going to provide us with a convenient manner of performing the manipulations that you need on your data.

3. This library will contain the functionality and methods to help us solve the variety of math problems with the help of linear algebra.

4. The operations that we are able to use on these arrays are going to be fast because they are natively written out in the C programming language.

5. In addition, many of the libraries that come with Python are going to need the arrays of NumPy to help them get things done.

How to Create NumPy Arrays

From here, we need to take some time to learn how to create these arrays. We will assume that you already have the NumPy library on your computer and ready to go. There are then two main ways that we are able to create some of these arrays including:

1. You can go through and make one of these arrays with the nested list or the Python list.

2. We can also work with some of the methods that are built-in with NumPy to make these arrays.

We are going to start out by looking at the steps that are necessary in order to create an array from the nested list and the Python list. To do this, we just need to pass the list from Python with the method of np.array() as your argument, and then you are done. When you do this, you will get either a vector or a 1D array, which can help you to get a lot of the necessary work done.

There are also times when we want to take this a bit further. We would want to get out of the 1D array that we just created, and we want to turn it into a 2D array or a matrix. To do this, we simply need to pass the Python list of lists to the method of np.array(), and then it is done for us.

The method above is simple to work with, and it will likely be enough to create the arrays that you want. Most beginners are going to start with this method because it helps them to take control of things, and it is not that complicated to work with. However, sometimes, we need to go through and do it a bit differently, or we want a bit more power behind the work that we do. That is why we are going to look at how we can create some of these arrays with a built-in method available with NumPy.

The first one is going to be the method form NumPy known as arranging (). Some of the things that we can remember about this array include:

1. It is going to be used to help us create some 1D arrays when we need them.

2. It is a good one to use when we would like to use the range function from Python to create one of our vectors in this library.

3. The method is able to take on a few parameters to get things done, including the step, stop, and start.

4. It is going to make sure that we get values returned that are evenly spaced within the interval that we use with it.

We can also work with the methods of zeros() and ones() based on our needs. These are going to allow us to create some different arrays in this library that are going to include zeros and ones. It is easy to work with, and we can code on them by simply writing out np.zeros() and np.ones() as the methods.

Another method that we can work with is the linspace. This is going to be used to help us create an array that has numbers that are equally spaced over the interval that you specify between two numbers. It is also able to accept a variety of arguments, including numbers, stop, and start. This one is also just going to create a vector or a 1D array for our needs.

These arrays are going to be important for us to work with. They allow us to have the ability to do a lot with our data and get it organized. In addition, since many of the other libraries in Python are going to rely on these arrays, and some of the other parts of the NumPy library to do their work, it is important to learn how this works and what makes these behave in the right manner as well.

Chapter 7: Saving NumPy Arrays

Now that we know a bit more about the NumPy arrays and what we can do with them, we need to take some time to learn about saving these so we can use them later. There are a number of methods that we can use when it is time to save these, and we just need to make sure that we are prepared to get this set up and ready to go. You can choose which method of saving the arrays that you would like to use based on your programming and the kind of data analysis that you would like to accomplish but let us look at some of the different ways that we can do it and the steps that will make them possible.

Saving Your NumPy Array to a .CSV File

The most common format that you will find when you would like to store this numerical data is going to be the CSV or comma-separated variable format. It is very likely that your training data and any of the data that you want to use, as an input to the models in this process will be stored in one of the CSV files. It is convenient and easy to use these and you would be able to use these to make some predictions from the model.

It is possible to save the arrays of NumPy to the CSV files with the help of the function of savext(). This function is going to help us take the array and the file name as the arguments so that we can save that array into the format of CSV if we would like. Remember that with this one, we need to be able to specify our delimiter, which is going to be the character that we use to separate all of the variables in the file, using a comma. This is going to be set with the delimiter argument to make things as easy as possible.

Let us look at an example of how we can use this and see how we are able to save our array with the.CSV file. The coding that we can use to make this happen includes:

 # save numpy array as CSV file

from numpy import asarray

from numpy import savetxt

 # define data

data = asarray([[0, 1, 2, 3, 4, 5, 6, 7, 8, 9]])

 # save to CSV file

savetxt('data.csv', data, delimiter=',')

Running this example is going to help us to not only define the array of NumPy but then we are going to be able to save it as a file known as data.csv. The array is going to have a single row of data that has ten columns in it. We would then expect that this data and all that goes with it would be saved to a CSV file, but it will be done with a single row of data. After running the example, it is possible for us to inspect all of the contents that are found with this file. We can then see that the data is going to be saved in the proper manner as a single row and that all of the flowing point numbers that we have in our array will be saved in full precision for us.

It is possible to look at another way to work with this kind of array as well. We are going to look at how to load our array from the CSV file that we are working with. We can take the data and load it up later as an array in NumPy with the help of the function of loadtext(). We need to remember that it is important to specify the filename and the same comma delimiter to make this work. The coding that we are able to use for this one is below:

load numpy array from CSV file

from numpy import loadtxt

```
# load array

data = loadtxt('data.csv', delimiter=',')

# print the array

print(data)
```

When we go through and run this example, it will load the data that is found in our CSV file and then print out the contents. This is going to help us to match our single row with the ten columns that we defined in the previous example.

Saving the NumPy Array to a Binary or .NPY File

The next thing that we are able to work with here is making sure that we save the array to a binary file. Sometimes we will have a ton of data that is found in our arrays, and we want to make sure that we save it quickly and efficiently. This means that we would want to work on saving the arrays into a native binary format so that it is efficient, both when we need to load and when we need to save them.

This is a common method to work with when the input data we must use has already been prepared ahead of time, such as transformed data that will need to be used for testing the models that we want to use in machine learning. In addition, it can be helpful for helping us run many experiments in the process. This file format of .npy is going to work well here and it is just known as the NumPy format. This can be achieved when we work with the function of save(), and then we just need to specify the filename and which array that we would like to save here.

Let us look at an example of how we are able to make this work. The example that we will list out below is going to help us to define a 2D array and then will make sure that we can save it as an .npy file.

```
# save numpy array as npy file
from numpy import asarray
from numpy import save
# define data
data = asarray([[0, 1, 2, 3, 4, 5, 6, 7, 8, 9]])
# save to npy file
save('data.npy', data)
```

After we have some time to run the example, we will see that there is a new file in the directory that comes with the name of data.npy. We are not able to directly go through and inspect the contents that are in this file with the text editor. This is because it is the format that is binary for now.

We can look at another example of doing this process and making sure that we load our NumPy array from this kind of file. We are able to load this whole file as an array with the help of the function of load(). The example that we are able to use to make this one happen includes:

 # load numpy array from npy file

from numpy import load

 # load array

data = load('data.npy')

 # print the array

print(data)

When you go through and run the example that is above, it will help us to load up the file and print the contents as you wish, and it will confirm for us that it was loaded in the right manner and that the content is going to match what we were expecting in that format as well.

How to Save the Array in a .NPZ File (Compressed)

The third way that we can save one of our arrays is in a compressed file. There are times when we are trying to prepare our data for modeling, and we need to have it set up to be reused across more than one experiment. However, when we do this, it is possible that our data is going to be large.

This might be something that we can pre-process into the array, like the corpus of text, or integers, or a collection of rescaled image data that would be the pixels. In these cases and more, it is possible and desirable that we would work to save it both to a regular data file, but also in a more compressed format, so it is easier to use.

When we work with the compressed format, it is going to allow some of the gigabytes of our data to be reduced to just hundreds, rather than many thousands, and can allow for an easier transmission process to some of the other servers or cloud computing for the long runs in algorithms. If this is something that you want to work with, then handling the .npz file format is going to be the best option for this case, and it is going to make sure that the right support for the compressed version of the native NumPy file format.

Another function that we can use with this one is going to be the savez_compressed(). This is a good one because it will automatically come in and make sure that we are able to save our arrays as just one single compressed file in this format if we wish.

With this in mind, we need to take a closer look at how to use this function to save some of our single NumPy arrays into a compressed file, making them easier to move around and use when they get really large. A good example of how we are able to work with this one is the code below:

save numpy array as npz file

from numpy import asarray

from numpy import savez_compressed

define data

```
data = asarray([[0, 1, 2, 3, 4, 5, 6, 7, 8, 9]])
# save to npy file
savez_compressed('data.npz', data)
```

When we run the example above, we will find that the example can define our array and then will get it to save it into a compressed file that has the name of data.npz. As with the format that we talked about earlier, we are not able to look through the contents of this saved file with the text editor that we are using because it is in a binary format.

Now, it is time for us to load the NumPy array from our NPZ file. We are able to load up this file at any time that we would like, as long as we use the function of load() as we did before. In this case, when we work with the function of savez_compressed(), we will find that it supports us saving more than one array to the save file. Then the load() function is going to help us to load many arrays as well.

The arrays that we are able to load here are going to be returned from our load() function in a dict, and then the names are going to be arr_0 for the first array, arr_1 for the second array, and so on in this order. To help us to load up the single array that we made earlier, we would want to use the coding from below:

```
# load numpy array from npz file
from numpy import load
# load dict of arrays
dict_data = load('data.npz')
# extract the first array
data = dict_data['arr_0']
# print the array
print(data)
```

If you take the time to run this example, you will find that it can load up the compressed file that you created and will contain all of the dictionaries of arrays that you saved. Then it is also going to be able to extract the very first array that we saved. In this case, we only saved one, so everything is going to print all of the information that is in there. With the first array, the program will print out the contents to help us confirm the values as well as the shape of the array so we can make sure that it matches up to the array that we saved to start with.

As we can see here, there are tons of things that we can do when it comes to working on the NumPy arrays. And being able to do at least a little bit of coding with this will ensure that we are set to go and can handle a lot of the work that we need, whether it is looking for data, cleaning the data, or creating some of our own algorithms along the way, with all of the other data science libraries out there.

Chapter 8: All About Matplotlib

It is now time for us to talk about a great library that you can work with when it is time to work on all of your visuals and more in this library. The best plotting library that we can use for all of our visuals and graphs and charts is known as matplotlib.

Matplotlib is going to be known as one of the plotting libraries that is available for the Python programming language, and it is going to rely on the NumPy library to give it the necessary arrays. This library is able to rely on object-oriented API to embed plots in Python applications. No matter how you want to be able to visualize your data over time, you will find that this is the library to get it all done.

Since Python is widely used in machine learning, resources like Matplotlib and NumPy are going to be useful to help us model out many of the technologies that we see with machine learning. The idea is that programmers would use both of these libraries to get some of the tasks down inside of a big environment of Python. Then, we can take those results and integrate them with all of the other features and elements that are inside of our machine learning program. It will also work with some advanced machines or even neural networks if we would like.

The utility of Matplotlib and NumPy has to do with numbers. The utility that we are able to find with matplotlib specifically will focus on some of the tools that we can use for visual plotting. Therefore, to keep it simple, these resources are going to be seen as more analytical than generative. However, all of the infrastructures work together to allow machine learning programs to produce results that are useful to those who need it in machine learning.

What is Matplotlib?

With some of that in mind, let us dive a bit more into what matplotlib is all about and how we can utilize this for some of our own needs as well. This is a plotting library that we will use for things like 2D graphs while working with machine learning and data analysis in the Python language. We can use it for many options like web application servers, python scripts, python scripts, and some of the other interface toolkits that are graphical.

A few toolkits that we can use are great for helping us to extend Python and the functionality that you will see with the Matplotlib library. Some of these are going to be separate downloads that you will have to add to your computer if you want to use them, while others are shipped at the same time with the source code of matplotlib, but they may have some external dependencies. Some of the options that you can use include:

1. **Basemap:** This is going to be a toolkit that we can use for plotting out different parts. It comes with many things like political boundaries, coastlines, and map projections.

2. **Cartopy:** Now we see that there is a mapping library featuring map projection definitions that are object-oriented, and some other capabilities to help you get the work done.

3. **Excel Tools:** This library is going to provide us with some of the utilities that we need to exchange all of our data with Microsoft Excel if we would like.

The Types of Plots

You can work with actually quite a few different plots and graphs. We can pick out the one that is best for our needs, and it depends on the kind of data that you want to work with, and how you can visualize this information the best as well. We are going to look at a few of the codes that you can use to create these plots and see the best results possible.

First, let us start out with a very basic plot that we are able to do in this library to generate a simple graph. Open up your compiler in Python and type in the code below to see how this can work:

```
from matplotlib import pyplot as plt

#Plotting to our canvas

plt.plot([1,2,3],[4,5,1])

#Showing what we plotted

plt.show()
```

Therefore, with just a few lines of code, you will be able to generate a basic graph with this kind of library. It is just that simple to work with. We can then take this simple code and add in a few other parts. We can add titles, labels, and more to the graph that is seen in the library in order to bring in some more meaning to it. We can use some of the codings that are below to do these things:

It is also possible to go through with this and try out some of the different styling techniques so that the graph is going to look the way that you would like. You could go through and change up the color or the width of a particular line in the graph, or you could add in a few grid lines if you would like. Therefore, we need to be able to learn how to add in some of the stylings when it comes to these graphs with matplotlib. First, remember that we need to be able to import the style package from our matplotlib library, and then we need to use the styling function to do the rest.

Now that we have been able to create a pretty basic code for a basic graph, we can go through and be a bit more specific about what we are doing on all of this and make it a little easier to handle. We are going to make our own bar graph in this library so that we can compare the data we have and more. A bar graph is going to work with bars so that we can compare the data that is found through different categories. It is going to be suited well when we want to be able to see how changes are going to happen over a certain period, based on what we want. You can make this bar graph go either vertically or horizontally. With this one, when you have a bar that is longer than the others are, it means that the value is higher. With this in mind, the coding that we need to use to make our bar graph is below:

```
from matplotlib import pyplot as plt

plt.bar([0.25,1.25,2.25,3.25,4.25],[50,40,70,80,20],
label="BMW",width=.5)
plt.bar([.75,1.75,2.75,3.75,4.75],[80,20,20,50,60],
label="Audi", color='r',width=.5)
plt.legend()
plt.xlabel('Days')
plt.ylabel('Distance (kms)')
plt.title('Information')
plt.show()
```

We can also take some of the same ideas and use them to make our own histogram. There is a difference present between the bar graph that we did above and a histogram. The histogram is going to be used to show distribution, but then the bar chart is going to be used to help us compare a few different entities to one another. These are going to be the most useful when you have arrays or a list that is long.

We are going to look at an example of how to make some of these for our own needs. We are going to do an example where we are able to plot out the population's age based on which bin they fall into. This bin is going to be important because it will consist of a range in most cases. The bins often want to be similar in size to one another to make them as even as possible. We are going to use the code below, which will give us intervals often. This means we work from 0 to 9, 10 to 19, and so on.

```
import matplotlib.pyplot as plt
population_age                                                    =
[22,55,62,45,21,22,34,42,42,4,2,102,95,85,55,110,120,70,65,55,1
11,115,80,75,65,54,44,43,42,48]
bins = [0,10,20,30,40,50,60,70,80,90,100]
plt.hist(population_age, bins, histtype='bar', rwidth=0.8)
plt.xlabel('age groups')
plt.ylabel('Number of people')
plt.title('Histogram')
plt.show()
```

Then it is time to work with scatter plots to help us compare some variables. Therefore, we will be able to use it to see how much one of our variables is affected by another variable so that we can take it and build up a new relation out of it. You can then take this data and make sure that it is out and on display more as a collection of the points rather than having them all come in with more than one variable to help determine where it will fall more on the axis that goes horizontal and then the value that we will see with the second variable that we have will help to determine the position when we look at the axis that is going more vertical.

The next thing that we are able to create with this library is known as an area plot. Area plots are going to be similar to what we will see with the line plot. We can also give these another name that is known as a stack plot. These kinds of plots are used well to track some of the changes that we want to know about over two or more groups that are supposed to be related and would fit into the same category. We could compile the work that was done during the day and put it into categories like working, eating, sleeping, and playing. The code that we are able to use for this one will be below:

import matplotlib.pyplot as plt
days = [1,2,3,4,5]

sleeping =[7,8,6,11,7]
eating = [2,3,4,3,2]

```
working =[7,8,7,2,2]
playing = [8,5,7,8,13]

plt.plot([],[],color='m', label='Sleeping', linewidth=5)
plt.plot([],[],color='c', label='Eating', linewidth=5)
plt.plot([],[],color='r', label='Working', linewidth=5)
plt.plot([],[],color='k', label='Playing', linewidth=5)

plt.stackplot(days,          sleeping,eating,working,playing,
colors=['m','c','r','k'])

plt.xlabel('x')
plt.ylabel('y')
plt.title('Stack Plot')
plt.legend()
plt.show()
```

While there are a lot of other graphs and charts that we are able to spend our time on, we are going to focus on the pie chart. The pie chart is simply going to be a circular kind of graph that will be made into some segments, which may look like the same slices that we see in a pie. This is a good way to work with our data because it can show us the data in terms of percentage so that it is easier to tell how important each one is, and will tell us more about a category. The coding that we can use to make this one work includes:

There are many graphs and more that we can utilize when it comes to using this library. It works well with the Python library and can be a great way to take all of the data that you are working within your data analysis and put it to good work. When you are ready to get started with the matplotlib library, take the time to look through this chapter and see some of the easy chartings and graphing that we are able to do to get it all done based on which chart and graph is the right for you.

Chapter 9: All About Pandas and IPython

Now it is time for us to take a closer look at some of the other things that we are able to do when it comes to working in the Python language, especially when we want to focus on the idea of data analysis and more. We are going to hone our attention on to the Pandas library and the IPython library to help us learn more about what we can do with both of them and how we can make them get our data sorted and ready to use. Let us dive right in and see how these will work.

Pandas

First, we are going to look at the Pandas library. Pandas are going to be a big name when we want to use the Python language to analyze the data we have, and it is actually one of the most used tools that we can bring out when it comes to data wrangling and data munging. Pandas are open-sourced, similar to what we see with some of the other libraries and extensions that are found in Python world. It is also free to use and will be able to handle all of the different parts of your data analysis.

There is a lot that you will enjoy when working with the Pandas library, but one of the neat things is that this library is able to take data, of almost any format that you would like, and then create a Python object out of it. This is known as a data frame and will have the rows and columns that you need to keep it organized. It is going to look similar to what we are used to seeing with an Excel sheet. When it is time to sort through our data and more, you will find that it is a lot easier to work with compared to some of the other options like loops or list comprehensions or even dictionaries.

As we mentioned, there are a variety of tasks that we can do when it comes to working with the Pandas library, but we are just going to focus on a few of them to give you an idea of how we can work on this and make it behave in the manner that we want. To start with, we are going to use this library to help us to load and save our data. When you want to use this particular library to help out with data analysis, you will find that you can use it in three different manners. These include:

1. You can use it to convert a Python dictionary or list, or aa array in NumPy to a data frame with the help of this library.

2. You can use it to open up a local file with Pandas. This is usually going to be done in a CSV file, but it is also possible to do it in other options like a delimited text file or in Excel.

3. You can also open a remote file or a database like JSON or CSV on one of the websites through a URL, or you can use it to read out the information that is found on an SQL table or database.

There are going to be a few different commands that show up with each of these options. However, when you want to open up a file, you would want to use the code of:

Pd read_filetype()

It is also possible for us to go through and use Pandas to view and inspect some of our data. You do not want just to gather the data and call it good. You want to be able to look through the data and inspect it as well. Once you have had some time to load the data, then it is time to look at it and see what is inside of that set of data. This allows us to see how the data frame is going to look.

To start with this one, running the name of the data frame would give you a whole table, but you can also go through and look at just the first n rows of your choice or the final rows as well. TO make this happen, we would just need to work with the codes of df.head(n) or df.tail(n). Depending on the code that you decide to use, it is possible to go through and look through a lot of information and figure out what is inside of there, and what data is going to be the most important for that.

Some of the other commands that you will be able to use in order to get the most out of the Pandas library and to ensure that we are going to be able to view and inspect your data will include:

1. **Df.mean():** This one is going to help us get back the means of all our columns.

2. **Df.corr():** This one is going to give us back the correlation between the different columns that are found in a data frame.

3. **Df.count():** This one is going to be helpful because it will give us back the number of values that are not considered null in each of the columns of the data frame.

4. **Df.max():** This one is going to provide us with the highest value in each column.

5. **Df.median():** This one is going to give us the median that we need in all of our columns.

6. **Df.std():** This is a good one to use because it will provide us with the standard deviation that is found in all of the columns.

These are just a few of the different things that we are able to do when it comes to using the Pandas library. This is a good way to help us to get all of the different data analysis parts done in a safe and effective manner. We can use it for all the different parts that come with data analysis, and if you combine it together with the arrays in NumPy, you can get some amazing results in the process.

IPython

Another environment that we can look at is the IPython environment. This is a bit different from some of the others, but it is going to help us to get some more work done. IPython is going to be a shell that is interactive and works well with the Python programming language. It is there to help us to work with many good source codes and can do some tab completion, work with some additional shell syntax, and enhanced introspection all on one.

This is going to be one of the alternatives that we can get with the Python interpreter. A shell is more interactive that can be used for some of the computing that you want to do in Python. In addition, it can provide us with more features based on what we would like to do with our work.

You can enjoy several features when working on the IPython environment. First, it will help you to run more shell commands that are native. When you run any of the interpreters that you would like to use, the interpreter should have a number of commands that are built-in. These commands are sometimes going to collide with the native commands of the shell.

For example, if we wanted to work with the traditional interpreter of Python and we typed in the code of "cd" after the interpreter loaded up, you would get an error on your screen. The reason for this error is that the interpreter is not going to recognize this command. This is a command that is native to the terminal of your computer, but not to the Python interpreter. On the other hand, IPython is going to have some more support for those native shell commands so you can utilize them in your work.

IPython is also a good one to work with when it comes to syntax highlighting. One of the first things that we are going to notice about this is that it provides us with syntax highlighting. This means that it is going to use color to help us look over the different parts of the Python code. If you type in x = 10 to your terminal, you would be able to see how the IPython environment is going to highlight this code in a variety of colors. The syntax highlighting is going to be a big improvement over what we see in the default interpreter of Python and can help us to read the code a bit better.

Another benefit of working with IPython is that it works with the proper indentation to help you out. If you have done some coding in the past, you know that it does pay attention to the indentation and whitespace. IPython recognizes this and then automatically provides you with the right indentation as you type the code into this interpreter. This makes things a lot easier as you go through the process.

This environment is also going to work with tab completion. IPython is going to provide us with some tab-completion so that we do not have to worry about handling this. This helps to ensure that the compiler is going to know what is going on with the codes that we write and that all of the work will show up in the manner that you want.

Documentation is another feature that we are able to see with IPython, and it is going to help us to work well with the code. Doing the autocompletion of tabs is going to be useful because it will provide us with a list of all the methods that are possible inside of the specific module. With all of the options at your disposal, you may be confused at what one particular method does. In addition, this is where the documentation of IPython can come into play. It will provide you with the documentation for any method you work with to save time and hassle.

Then the final benefit that we are going to look at here is that IPython can help with pasting blocks of code. IPython is going to be excellent when we want to paste large amounts of Python code. You can grab any block of the Python code, paste it into this environment, and you should get the result of a code that is properly indented and ready to go on this environment. It is as easy as all that.

You can see that there are many different benefits that come with the IPython environment. You can choose to work with the regular Python environment if you would like, but there are also many benefits to upgrading and working with this one as well, especially when you are working with something like data science and completing your own data analysis.

Both the IPython environment and the Pandas libraries are going to be useful when it is time to handle some of our data analysis and can ensure we have the right codes present in order to complete those projects. In addition, when we combine them with some of the great features of the NumPy library and the matplotlib library, we will be able to go through and handle any data analysis project that we want along the way.

Chapter 10: Using Python Data Analysis with Practical Examples

Now we are going to look at a quick example of how we can complete a bit of the data analysis that we want to do with Python. We are going to complete some of our work with the help of the Pandas library that we talked about before to help us get this one done. Keep in mind that this is just a quick example, there are many other parts that can come into play, and it is possible that the data analysis you want to complete is going to be more complex.

Make sure to open up the notebook that you would like to use for this. You can stick with the traditional Python environment to get things done, or you can choose to work with the IPython as we chose before. The first thing that we need to do with this is to make sure that we import the right libraries. Just because they are on your computer does not mean the code knows that you want to work with them. Instead, you need to bring them in so that the code knows you mean to use them.

For this project, we are going to work with two main libraries, the panda's library, and the NumPy library. The code that we can use to make these come out and work for us include:

```
import pandas as pd
import numpy as np
```

When that is done, we can go through and read some of the sample data that will help us to create our analysis. We also want to be able to get a good summary of how this is going to look. Some of the codings that we need to use here include the following:

```
SALES=pd.read_csv("sample-sales.csv")
SALES.head()
```

Take some time to go through this and run the compiler so that you can see what is going to show up, and how the information is going to look. You should get a nice table that has all of the necessary data to make this easier.

When this is all done, we are able to go on to the next step. We want to use what is known as the function of a pivot table. This is going to be used to help us summarize the sales and then will turn the rows of data into something that we are able to use. Since this is our first project, we are going to keep it as simple as possible so work with the code below:

```
report                                          =
SALES.pivot_table(values=['quantity'],index=['Account
Name'],columns=['category'], aggfunc=np.sum)

report.head(n=10)
```

When we do this, we are going to be able to do a few more things. This particular command is going to show us the number of products that all of our customers have been able to purchase, and it all shows up in just that one command.

While this is something that is impressive, you may notice when you look at the output that there are a number of NaN's in the output. This is going to stand for Not a Number and will show us where there is not a value in place for us to work with. In many cases, we want to change this so that it says something like 0 instead of the NaN. We can do this with the function of fill_value as we see in the code below:

```
report =
SALES.pivot_table(values=['quantity'],index=['Account
Name'],columns=['category'], fill_value=0, aggfunc=np.sum)
report.head(n=10)
```

When you check out the output on this one, it should be a little bit nicer and cleaner to look at. We are going to then take this to one more step before we finish up. This will help us to see some more of the power that will show up with the pivot_table. For this one, we are going to work with some coding that will show us how much ins ales we were able to do:

```
report = SALES.pivot_table(values=['ext
price','quantity'],index=['Account Name'],columns=['category'],
fill_value=0,aggfunc=np.sum)
report.head(n=10)
```

It is even possible for us to take all of this and output it to Excel. We do need to go through a few steps to make this happen, such as converting all of the information back to our DataFrame.

Then it can be written out to work in Excel. The code that we can use for this one is below:

```
report.to_excel ('report.xlsx', sheet_name='Sheet1')
```

That is as simple as this process is. We can utilize some of the codes that are present with the Python language in order to get them to behave in the right manner, and you will find that it makes things a whole lot easier to do in the end. You can add in more parts and make it more complicated as well, but overall, these are the basics of what we can do when it comes to working with this process.

Chapter 11: Essential Tools with Python Data Analysis

Before we are able to get too far in some of our work with the Python data analysis, though, we need to make sure that we know what some of the essential tools are all about, and how to use all of these. The more that we know about some of the tools and how they work, the more that we will be able to get out of our data analysis overall. This makes it a lot easier for us to feel good about our work, and to use it in the proper manner to make some smart decisions along the way.

The neat thing about doing this analysis with the help of the Python language is that there are already a ton of tools and methods that come with it. You can pick out another language for the power or some other feature, but when you want many options, and you want the ability to work with ton of different parts, with your analysis, then Python is the way to go.

We already took some time to talk about a few of the tools that are available when it comes to this Python data analysis. You are not going to get too far, for example, if you are not working with the NumPy library, the Pandas library, and the IPython environment. However, there are whole hosts of other options and tools that you are able to bring in to ensure you get the most out of this whole process. Some of the other tools that work so well with Python data analysis will include:

GraphLab Create

The first tool that we are going to use is the GraphLab Create. This is considered a Python library that has been backed by the C++ engine. It is a good one to help us build up a large-scale and even higher in performance when we are working with our products that relate to date. The neat thing here is that there are many features that will show up with this tool, and some of the ones that pertain to us the most include:

1. The ability to analyze some of the terabyte-scale data at speeds that allow for interaction, right from your own desktop.

2. It can work with a single platform so we can work on images, text, graphs, and tabular data of our choice if we would like.

3. It works with a lot of the most common, and some of the more state of the art, machine learning algorithms,

including things like factorization machines, boosted trees, and deep learning, to name a few.

4. It is going to run the same code, whether you are doing this on a distributed system or if you are on a laptop. The programming or the software that you use with it is not going to matter all that much either.

5. It helps you to focus on some of the tasks that you want to, along with some of the machine learning, with flexible API.

6. It helps to deploy some of your data products in the cloud with the help of Predictive Services.

7. It is also good for visualizing data so that you are able to complete some exploration and even do production monitoring, as you would like.

Scikit-Learn

You are not going to get too far when it comes to working on a data analysis if you do not bring in the Scikit-Learn library. This is going to be seen as one of the simple and efficient tools that you can use for data mining and for completing data analysis. What is so great about this one is that it is going to be accessible to anyone, and it can be reusable in many contexts as well. In addition, it is built on some of the other libraries that we have talked about, including matplotlib, SciPy, and NumPy. It is also going to come to us with a commercially usable license and it is open source, so we are able to work with it and use it in the manner that we want. Some of the features that we are likely to see with this one include:

1. It can help with problems of classification. This is where it helps us to identify which category a particular object is going to belong with.

2. It can help with some problems of regression. This is where it is able to predict a continuous value attribute associated with the object.

3. It can help with some problems with clustering. This is where we are going to have an automatic grouping of objects that are similar in the sets.

4. It can help us complete something that is known as dimensionality reduction. This is where we are able to reduce the number of random variables that we want to normalize in all of this.

Spark

Another option that we can focus on is known as Spark. This is going to be made up of a driver program that will run some of the main functions of the user and can then execute the various parallel operations on our chosen cluster. One of the main abstractions that we are going to see in Spark is that it provides us with an RDD or a distributed set of data that is resilient. This is going to be elements that are in a collection but which are supposed to be partitioned through the nodes of that cluster and with which we are able to operate them in parallel to one another.

You will find that these RDDs are created when we start with one of the files that is on the system, whether you are doing it on Scala or Hadoop, and then we take the right steps in order to transform it. Users can sometimes use this tool to persist in the memory of RDD. This helps them to reuse that part of the code efficiently through parallel operations. In addition to all of this, the RDDs will automatically recover from the node failures that show you as well.

A second abstraction is going to be known as the shared variables. This is going to be used in parallel operations. When we look at the default, when Spark is able to run a function in parallel as a set of tasks that happen on the different nodes, it is going to ship one of the copies of all the variables that we want to use in order to get the function to behave in the manner that we would like.

You may find during all of this that the variable is something that we need to share through more tasks, or between the programs that is the program and all of the other tasks that your company needs to do. Spark is a good option because it has been able to share the types of variables that we can work with. This can be the broadcast variable, which is what we are going to use to help us cache a value in the memory of all the nodes. Alternatively, we can use the accumulators, which are going to be variables that are only added to the mix, such as the sums and the counters.

Tableau Public

We are also able to work with this option, as it is a simple and intuitive tool that will help us to get as many insights as we can with the help of data visualizations. This has a million-row limit, which means that it will work so much better than some of the other options that you can make in the world of data analytics.

When you utilize some of the visuals that come with this tool, it helps you to explore some of your data, do an exploration of your hypothesis, and even double-check some of the insights that you have.

We can work with this tool many ways. For example, it is able to the public some of the more interactive data visuals to the web and it will do it all free for you. In addition, you do not need to have many programming skills to get it done. Visualizations that are published with this one can be embedded into the web pages and the blogs, and you can even share them through social media or email. The shared content can be made available for you and for others to download if you would like.

OpenRefine

Another option that we are going to look at is known as OpenRefine. This was originally known as GoogleRefine, but it is known as a data cleaning software that will help you to clean up your data, so it is ready to go through the analysis. It is going to operate on a row of data that will have cells under the columns, and it is similar to what we see with any relational database that the company may have used in the past.

There are a number of ways that we can utilize this kind of tool. To start with, it is going to be useful when we need to clean up some of the messy data. It is also good for transforming the data and parse the data from the websites that you found it on. In addition, it is going to work by adding some more data to a dataset by fetching it from web services. For example, this tool could be used to geocode addresses to the right coordinates geographically.

KNIME

We can also work with an option that is known as KNIME. This is considered one of the top tools in data analytics because it is there to help us to manipulate, analyze, and model data through some visual programming. It is going to be used to help integrate some of the different components for data mining and machine learning through some of the concepts, including the one about modular data pipelining.

With this program, instead of going through and writing out blocks of code, you just need to go through and drop and drag connection points between the activities that you are trying to use. This data analysis tool will support a number of programming languages like Python, and you can use many different analysis tools so that they can run data for chemistry, do text mining, and more in the Python language.

Dataiku DSS

In addition, the final tool on our list that we are going to look at here is known as Dataiku DSS. This is a good software platform that your whole team can love. A collaborative data science software program will allow everyone on your team some time to build, explore, prototype, and deliver some of their own products with data in the most efficient manner possible.

There are many ways that we are able to use this kind of software. First, it is going to provide us with an interactive visual interface where they can point, click, and build. Moreover, you can even bring some of the other coding languages into it to help get things done.

This particular tool is going to be useful with our data analysis because it will help us to do a draft on our data preparation and then move it all to the modulization in just a few seconds. It can work by helping to coordinate the development and operations when it handles the automation of workflow, creates some predictive web services, model health on a frequent basis, such as daily, and will even help to monitor data.

All of these tools can come together to help us get all of our work done in data analysis. Whether we are working with the Python language or we want to utilize these tools to help get the work done, it is important that we really learn how to make this work and what we are able to do to see some great results in the process. Look at some of these great tools and see how they can help you see the results that you want in no time.

Chapter 12: Data Visualization

Before we can finish off our own data analysis, we need to take some time to learn about data visualization and how we are able to utilize this for some of our needs. These visuals are amazing because they can take all of the data that we have collected and sorted through and analyzed from before and puts it into a format that we can read and understand. Visuals and graphs are a whole lot easier to look through and gain the main meaning from than reading through reports and spreadsheets, which is why these data visuals are going to be such an important part of this process. With this in mind, we are going to dive in and take a look at the data visualizations and what we are able to do with them.

The Background of Data Visualization

To start with, we need to understand that data visualization is just going to be the presentation of data in a graphical or a pictorial format. It is going to enable some decision-makers to look through the analytics that we did with all of our data, but it is done in a visual manner. This will help everyone involved grasp difficult concepts or identify some new patterns that are important. Moreover, we even have the chance to work with visualizations that are a bit more interactive, which helps us to take this concept a bit further. This helps us to use a lot of our modern technology in order to drill down into the charts and graphs to find more details and can help us to change the data we see interactively, and process it to meet our needs.

With that information in mind, it is time for us to look a bit at some of the histories that are possible with data visuals. The concept of using pictures and graphs to look through data and understand it a bit more has been around for centuries. For example, how many times did travelers and even those who have gone to war worked with maps to help them see what is going on and to figure out what they did next?

Visuals can help us to figure out what kind of business we are looking at, can help us to separate out things in a group, and can even help with making maps and working with things like temperatures and geographical features that we need as well. This is a big reason why we would want to work with these to help with our data visualization.

The technology that comes in our modern world has really lit a big fire under data visualization and how it works for our needs. Computers have made it possible to go through and process a huge amount of data, and we are able to do it at incredibly high speeds as well. Moreover, because of this, we can see that data visualizations is a big blend of art and science that is already having a large impact over the corporate landscape over the next few years.

There are a lot of ways that we are able to work with these data visuals, and taking the time to learn how to use them, and to learn all of the different ways that you can work with these to help you understand what data you are taking in and what it means for you, can make all of the difference in how well you can use your own data.

Why is Data Visualization so Important?

Now that we have had a chance to talk about data visualizations a bit, it is important to understand why this is something that is so important. Why can't we just go through the analysis and then understand the information that is there? There are many reasons why you should work with the data analysis and why it is such an important part of the process that you should focus on.

Due to the way that the brain is able to take in information and process it, using charts or graphs to help visualize some of the large amounts of data, especially the kind that is more complex, is going to be a lot easier compared to pouring over spreadsheets and reports. Data visualization is going to be one of the quick and easy methods that help to convey all of these concepts in an easy to understand manner.

Think about how much you are able to fit into one of these visuals. Even language barriers are not such a big deal because we know what is found in the data just by looking at the image. And we can use one image to tell us a lot about the process and the data that we are working with, something that could take up pages of complicated jargon to do when we work with it on a spreadsheet or another document. This is all possible and easy to work with when we work on extensions to the Python language, such as the Matplotlib library that we talked about before.

In addition to some of the topics that we discussed above, there are a few other ways that we are able to work with data visualization. Some of these are going to include:

1. The data visuals are going to help us to figure out which areas in our business are more likely toned some improvement and some of our attention.

2. These data visuals are going to help us to clarify which factors are more likely to influence the behavior of other customers.

3. These data visuals are going to make it easier to understand which products should be placed in different locations.

4. When they are used in the proper manner, these data visuals are going to be able to help a company predict their volume of sales so that they can do other things inside of the business to reduce waste and make more money.

Moreover, these are just a few of the things that the data visuals are going to be able to do for us. Moreover, with all of the different options that we can choose when it comes to working with data visuals, from pie charts, bar graphs, and so much more. This helps us to handle any and all of the data that we want in a safe and secure manner, while really seeing what information is hidden inside of it.

How Can We Use Data Visualization?

The next thing that we need to look at here is how these visuals are being used in the first place. No matter how big the industry is, all businesses are working with data visualization to help them make more sense of their data overall. In addition, there are varieties of methods that can be used to help with this one. Some of the ways that companies are working with data visualizations include:

It can help them to comprehend the information they are working with much better. By using graphs for the information of the business, it is easier for these companies to see a large amount of data in a manner that is more cohesive and clear. Moreover, they can then draw better conclusions from that information. Moreover, because it is always a lot easier for the brain to analyze information in a format that is graphic, rather than looking through spreadsheets and other methods, businesses are able to address problems and even answer questions in a more timely manner.

How to Lay the Groundwork

Before you take some time to implement some new technology, there are a number of steps that all businesses need to be able to take. Not only do you need to have a nice solid grasp on the data at hand, but we also need to be able to understand our goals, needs, and the audience we are working with. Preparing your organization for the technology that has to come with these data visuals is going to require that we can do the following first:

1. We need to have a good understanding of the data that we want to visualize. This includes the size and how unique the values in the charts are going to be to one another.

2. We need to be able to determine what we would like to visualize and what information we are hoping to communicate when we pick out a chart or a graph to use.

3. We need to have a good understanding of our audience and then understand how this audience is going to process information in a visual manner.

4. We need to use some visuals that can convey the information in the best and the simplest form that we can

so that our audience is able to understand what is going on.

Once you have been able to meet some of these needs about the data you are working with and the audience who you plan to consume your products, then it is time for us to get prepared for data we would like to work with. Big data is going to bring in new challenges to the work of visualization because we are able to see some of the larger volumes and the varieties that are there. Even some of the changes in the velocities are going to be important when we work here so we cannot forget all about this. In addition, the data that we will use can be generated in a much faster than we can analyze it and manage it in most cases.

We can then use this to help pinpoint some emerging trends that will show up in the data. Working on these kinds of visuals is a good idea because it will help us to find some of the trends that are in the market, and some of the business trends that are important. When we can find these, and we use them in the right way, it helps us to get the most out of our competition. Moreover, of course, this is a good way to affect your bottom line as well. It is easier to spot some of the outliers that would affect the quality of the product or some of the customer churn, and then you can address these issues before they turn into a bigger problem.

Identify some of the patterns and relationships that will show up. Even extensive amounts of data that may seem complicated to go through can make more sense when you present it in a graphical format. Moreover, you will find that businesses using this can find all of the parameters that are there and how much they will correlate with one another. You will find that a few of these are going to be obvious, and you may not need this data analysis to get it to work, but others are harder to find. The graphs and charts that you want to use can help the company focus on the best areas, the ones that are the most likely to influence their goals the most.

Finally, these visuals are going to be good at communicating the story to others. Once the business has been able to go through and uncover some new insights from these analytics, the next part of the process will include what we need in order to talk about these insights and show what they are to others. It is possible to work with charts and even some graphs and any of the some of the other representations that are impactful and fun to look at because it can engage and can help to get the message across as quickly as possible.

As we can see here, there are a lot of benefits to working with these visuals, and being able to add them to your data analysis is going to make a big difference overall. Companies in all industries are able to go through and work with some of the visuals to help them understand the data that they are analyzing in a manner that is easier than anything else is. You cannot go wrong adding in some of these visuals to your work and ensuring that you can fully understand what is going on in your data.

There are many factors that someone who is working with data analysis needs to worry about before they make some of their own charts and graphs to work with along the way. This can include things like the cardinality of the columns that they want to visualize. When we are dealing with a higher level of cardinality, it means that there are many unique values present, and it is possible that each user has different values. If you are working with something like gender, then your cardinality is going to be lower because there are two options.

These data visuals are going to be so important to ensure that we can work with some of our data in the most effective manner possible. It can help us to take that data and see what is inside of it, rather than worrying about trying to read the documents and spreadsheets that come with this. All data analysis should include some of these visuals to help us understand the data at hand a little bit easier.

Chapter 13: Applications of Data Analysis

Before we are done with this guidebook, we need to look at some of the applications that will help us to get the most out of data analysis. There are already so many ways that this data analysis is going to be used, and when we can put it all together, we are going to see some amazing results in the process. Places like the financial world, security, marketing, advertising, and healthcare are all going to benefit from this data analysis, and as more time goes on, it is likely that we will see more of these applications as well. Some of the ways that we are able to work with data analysis and get the best results from it include:

Security

There are several cities throughout the world that are working on predictive analysis so that they can predict the areas of the town where there is more likely to be a big surge for crime that is there. This is done with the help of some data from the past and even data on the geography of the area.

This is actually something that a few cities in America have been able to use, including Chicago. Although we can imagine that it is impossible to use this to catch every crime that is out there, the data that is available from using this is going to make it easier for police officers to be present in the right areas at the right times to help reduce the rates of crime in some of those areas. And in the future, you will find that when we use data analysis in this kind of manner in the big cities has helped to make these cities and these areas a lot safer, and the risks would not have to put their lives at risk as much as before.

Transportation

The world of transportation is able to work with data analysis, as well. A few years ago, when plans were being made at the London Olympics, there was a need during this event to handle more than 18 million journeys that were made by fans into the city of London. Moreover, it was something that we were able to sort out well.

How was this feat achieved for all of these people? The train operators and the TFL operators worked with data analytics to make sure that all those journeys went as smoothly as possible. These groups were able to go through and input data from the events that happened around that time and then used this as a way to forecast how many people would travel to it. This plan went so well that all of the spectators and the athletes could be moved to and from the right places in a timely manner the whole event.

Risk and Fraud Detection

This was one of the original uses of data analysis and was often used in the field of finance. There are many organizations that had a bad experience with debt, and they were ready to make some changes to this. Because they had a hold on the data that was collected each time that the customer came in for a loan, they were able to work with this process in order to not lose as much money in the process.

This allowed the banks and other financial institutions to dive and conquer some of the data from the profiles they could use from those customers. When the bank or financial institution is able to utilize their customers they are working with, the costs that had come up recently, and some of the other information that is important for these tools, they will make some better decisions about who to loan out money to, reducing their risks overall. This helps them to offer better rates to their customers.

In addition to helping these financial institutions make sure that they can hand out loans to customers who are more likely to pay them back, you will find that this can be used in order to help cut down on the risks of fraud as well. This can cost the bank billions of dollars a year and can be expensive to work with. When the bank can use all of the data that they have for helping discover transactions that are fraudulent and making it easier for their customers to keep money in their account, and make sure that the bank is not going to lose money in the process as well.

Logistics of Deliveries

There are no limitations when it comes to what we are able to do with our data analysis, and we will find that it works well when it comes to logistics and deliveries. There are several companies that focus on logistics, which will work with this data analysis, including UPS, FedEx, and DHL. They will use data in order to improve how efficient their operations are all about.

From applications of analytics of the data, it is possible for these companies who use it to find the best and most efficient routes to use when shipping items, the ones that will ensure the items will be delivered on time, and so much more. This helps the item to get things through in no time, and keeps costs down to a minimum as well. Along with this, the information that the companies are able to gather through their GPS can give them more opportunities in the future to use data science and data analytics.

Customer Interactions

Many businesses are going to work with the applications of data analytics in order to have better interactions with their customers. Companies can do a lot about their customers, often with some customer surveys. For example, many insurance companies are going to use this by sending out customer surveys after they interact with their handler. The insurance company is then able to use which of their services are good, that the customers like, and which ones they would like to work on to see some improvements.

There are many demographics that a business is able to work with and it is possible that these are going to need many diverse methods of communication, including email, phone, websites, and in-person interactions. Taking some of the analysis that they can get with the demographics of their customers and the feedback that comes in, it will ensure that these insurance companies can offer the right products to these customers, and it depends one hundred percent on the proven insights and customer behavior as well.

City Planning

One of the big mistakes that is being made in many places is that analytics, especially the steps that we are talking about in this guidebook, is not something that is being used and considered when it comes to city planning. Web traffic and marketing are actually the things that are being used instead of the creation of buildings and spaces. This is going to cause many of the issues that are going to come up when we talk about the power over our data is because there are some influences over building zoning and creating new things along the way in the city.

Models that have been built well are going to help maximize the accessibility of specific services and areas while ensuring that there is not the risk of overloading significant elements of the infrastructure in the city at the same time. This helps to make sure there is a level of efficiency as everyone, as much as possible, is able to get what they want without doing too much to the city and causing harm in that manner.

We will usually see buildings that are not put in the right spots or businesses that are moved where they do not belong. How often have you seen a building that was on a spot that looked like it was suitable and good for the need, but which had a lot of negative impact on other places around it? This is because these potential issues were not part of the consideration during the planning period. Applications of data analytics, and some modeling, helps us to make things easier because we will know what would happen if we put that building or another item on that spot that you want to choose.

Healthcare

The healthcare industry has been able to see many benefits from data analysis. There are many methods, but we are going to look at one of the main challenges that hospitals are going to face. Moreover, this is that they need to cope with cost pressures when they want to treat as many patients as possible while still getting high-quality care to the patients. This makes the doctors and other staff fall behind in some of their work on occasion, and it is hard to keep up with the demand.

You will find that the data we can use here has risen so much, and it allows the hospital to optimize and then track the treatment of their patient. It is also a good way to track the patient flow and how the different equipment in the hospital is being used. In fact, this is so powerful that it is estimated that using this data analytics could provide a 1 percent efficiency gain, and could result in more than $63 billion in worldwide healthcare services. Think of what that could mean to you and those around you.

Doctors are going to work with data analysis in order to provide them with a way to help their patients a bit more. They can use this to make some diagnosis and understand what is going on with their patients in a timely and more efficient manner. This can allow doctors to provide their customers with a better experience and better care while ensuring that they can keep up with everything they need to do.

Travel

Data analytics and some of their applications are a good way to help optimize the buying experience for a traveler. This can be true through a variety of options, including data analysis of mobile sources, websites, or social media. The reason for this is because the desires and the preferences of the customer can be obtained from all of these sources, which makes companies start to sell out their products thanks to the correlation of all the recent browsing on the site and any of the currency sells to help purchase conversions. They are able to utilize all of this to offer some customized packages and offers. The applications of data analytics can also help to deliver some personalized travel recommendations, and it often depends on the outcome that the company is able to get from their data on social media.

Travel can benefit other ways when it comes to working with the data analysis. When hotels are trying to fill up, they can work with data analysis to figure out which advertisements they would like to offer to their customers. Moreover, they may try to utilize this to help figure out which nights, and which customers, will fill up or show up. Pretty much all of the different parts of the travel world can benefit when it comes to working with data analysis.

Digital Advertising

Outside of just using it to help with some searching another, there is another area where we are able to see a data analytics happen regularly, and this is digital advertisements. From some of the banners that are found on several websites to the digital billboards that you may be used to seeing in some of the bigger and larger cities, but all of these will be controlled thanks to the algorithms of our data along the way.

This is a good reason why digital advertisements are more likely to get a higher CTR than the conventional methods that advertisers used to rely on a lot more. The targets are going to work more on the past behaviors of the users, and this can make for some good predictions in the future.

The importance that we see with the applications of data analytics is not something that we can overemphasize because it is going to be used in pretty much any and all of the areas of our life to ensure we have things go a bit easier than before. It is easier to see now, more than ever, how having data is such an important thing because it helps us to make some of the best decisions without many issues. However, if we don't have that data or we are not able to get through it because it is a mess and doo many points to look at, then our decisions are going to be based on something else. Data analysis ensures that our decisions are well thought out, that they make sense, and that they will work for our needs.

You may also find that when we inefficiently handle our data, it could lead to a number of problems. For example, it could lead to some of the departments that are found in a larger company so that we have a better idea of how we can use the data and the insights that we are able to find in the process, which could make it so that the data you have is not able to be used to its full potential. Moreover, if this gets too bad, then it is possible that the data will not serve any purpose at all.

However, you will find that as data is more accessible and available than ever before, and therefore more people, it is no longer just something that the data analysts and the data scientists are able to handle and no one else. Proper use of this data is important, but everyone is able to go out there and find the data they want. Moreover, this trend is likely to continue long into the future as well.

Conclusion

Thank you for making it through to the end of *Python Data Analysis*, let's hope it was informative and able to provide you with all of the tools you need to achieve your goals whatever they may be.

The next step is to start working on your own data analysis. So many companies can benefit when it comes to working with data analysis. Moreover, there are varieties of applications that we can use for this one as well. Learning how to work with this one is important to get the most out of it, and will ensure that we can make some smart decisions, learn more about our customers, and so much more.

There are many parts that come with our data analysis, and we are going to spend some time talking about many of them inside of this guidebook. And we will look at how we are able to do it with the help of the Python coding language. When we can bring together the efficiency and the amazing features of data analysis with the ease of use and power that comes with the Python language, you will find that it is so good for your business and helping you to make some smart decisions along the way.

After we had an introduction with the Python language and what data analysis is all about, along with some of the basics of the data science lifecycle, it is then time to move into some of the other parts that will show up with this process as well. We can look at some of the most important libraries that we will do with Python and data analysis, and then we can explore how to work with data visualizations, some of the ways to complete our own data analysis with some coding, and even how to do some of the other great parts of this data analysis as well.

There are so many things that we need to work in order to get the successful data analysis that we have hoped for. It is a process that takes some good time, and you have to have the dedication and time to get it all done. However, this guidebook will show us the right steps to make that happen as quickly and efficiently as possible. When you are ready to learn a bit more about data analysis and how to utilize it with the help of the Python language, make sure to check out this guidebook to help you out.

Finally, if you found this book useful in any way, a review on Amazon is always appreciated!

Python for Data Science

A Crash Course for Data Science and Analysis, Python Machine Learning and Big Data

Introduction

Congratulations on purchasing *Python for Data Science: A Python Crash Course for Data Science, Data Analysis, Python Machine Learning and Big Data* and thank you for doing so.

The following chapters will discuss the fundamental concepts of Data Science driven by the Python programming language to provide you a holistic understanding of all the latest cutting edge technologies. In the first chapter, you will learn the basics of data science technology with an in-depth overview of the most widely used data science lifecycle called Team Data Science Process (TDSP). The five major stages of the TDSP lifecycle that outline the interactive steps required for project execution have been described from start to finish along with the deliverables created at each stage. To help you build a solid understanding of various technologies, the core concept of different types of data has been described with examples. The difference between the process of data analysis and data science has also been provided to avoid any confusion between them as these terms are often used interchangeably.

Chapter 2, entitled "Introduction to Python Coding," will help you master this extremely intuitive and flexible programming language that can be used for a variety of coding projects, including machine learning algorithms, web applications, data mining and visualization, game development. With the provide installation instructions for Python, you will be able to download and install Python on your operating system and get hands-on code development experience. Some of the Python coding concepts described in this chapter include data types, variables, numbers, constructor functions, strings, Booleans, classes and objects among others. Each concept is explained with examples and exercises so you can learn and test your learning at the same time.

Chapter 3, entitled "Data Visualization and Analysis with Python," deals with the concept of big data analytics and the functioning of big data. The different steps involved in big data analysis are explained in detail. The terms data analysis and data visualization are increasingly being used synonymously but this book will help you understand the distinction between the two with the use and application of some of the most popular Python-based libraries. Scikit-Learn has evolved as the gold standard for machine learning and data analysis with Matplotlib offering visualization tools and science computing modules supported by SciPy. You will learn how to create various graphs using matplotlib and Pandas library.

The final chapter of this book explores the concepts of machine learning and predictive analysis. Machine learning allows the analysis of large volumes of data and delivers faster and more accurate results. There are four different machine learning algorithms that can be used to cater to the available data set and create a desired machine learning model. A variety of real life examples of the application of machine learning technology have been provided to help you understand the importance of machine learning in the modern world. Today companies are digging through their past with an eye on the future and this is where artificial intelligence for marketing comes into play, with the application of predictive analytics technology. This chapter will provide you explicit details on how companies are able to employ a predictive analytics model to gain an understanding of how their customers are interacting with their products or services based on their feelings or emotions shared on the social media platforms.

There are plenty of books on this subject on the market, thanks again for choosing this one! Every effort was made to ensure it is full of as much useful information as possible; please enjoy!

Chapter 1: Foundational Data Science Technologies

In the world of technology, Data is defined as "information that is processed and stored by a computer." Our digital world has flooded our realities with data. From a click on a website to our smart phones tracking and recording our location every second of the day, our world is drowning in the data. From the depth of this humongous data, solutions to our problems that we have not even encountered yet could be extracted. This very process of gathering insights from a measurable set of data using mathematical equations and statistics can be defined as "data science." The role of data scientists tends to be very versatile and is often confused with a computer scientist and a statistician. Essentially anyone, be it a person or a company that is willing to dig dcep to large volumes of data to gather information, can be referred to us data science practitioners. For example, companies like Walmart keeps track of and record of in-store and online purchases made by the customers, to provide personalized recommendations on products and services. The social media platforms like Facebook that allow users to list their current location is capable of identifying global migration patterns by analyzing the wealth of data that is handed to them by the users themselves.

The earliest recorded use of the term data science goes back to 1960 and credited to "Peter Naur," who reportedly used the term data science as a substitute for computer science and eventually introduced the term "datalogy." In 1974, Naur published a book titled "Concise Survey of Computer Methods," with liberal use of the term data science throughout the book. In 1992, the contemporary definition of data science was proposed at "The Second Japanese-French Statistics Symposium," with the acknowledgment of emergence of a new discipline focused primarily on types, dimensions and structures of data.

"Data science continues to evolve as one of the most promising and in-demand career paths for skilled professionals. Today, successful data professionals understand that they must advance past the traditional skills of analyzing large amounts of data, data mining, and programming skills. In order to uncover useful intelligence for their organizations, data scientists must master the full spectrum of the data science life cycle and possess a level of flexibility and understanding to maximize returns at each phase of the process."
– University of California, Berkley

An increasing interest by business executives has significantly contributed to the recent rise in popularity of the term data science. However, a large number of journalists and academic experts, do not acknowledge data science as a separate area of study from the field of statistics. A group within the same community considers data science is the popular term for "data mining" and "big data." The very definition of data science is up for debate within the tech community. The field of study that requires a combination of skill set including computer programming skills, domain expertise, and proficiency in statistics and mathematical algorithms to be able to extract valuable insight from large volumes of raw data is referred to as data science.

Data Science Lifecycle

The most highly recommended lifecycle to structured data science projects, the "Team Data Science Process" (TDSP). This process is widely used for projects that require the deployment of applications based on artificial intelligence and/or machine learning algorithms. It can also be customized for and used in the execution of "exploratory data science" projects as well as "ad hoc analytics" projects. The TDSP lifecycle is designed as an agile and sequential iteration of steps that serve as guidance on the tasks required for the use of predictive models. These predictive models need to be deployed in the production environment of the company, so they can be used in the development of artificial intelligence based applications. The aim of this data science lifecycle is high speed delivery and completion of data science projects toward a defined engagement end point. Seamless execution of any data science project requires effective communication of tasks within the team as well as to the stakeholders.

The fundamental components of the "Team Data Science Process" are:

Definition of a data science lifecycle

The five major stages of the TDSP lifecycle that outline the interactive steps required for project execution from start to finish are: "Business understanding," "Data acquisition in understanding," "modeling," "deployment" and "customer acceptance." Keep reading for details on this to come shortly!

Standardized Project Structure

To enable seamless and easy access to project documents for the team members allowing for quick retrieval of information, use of templates, and a shared directory structure goes a long way. All project documents and the project code our store and a "version control system" such as "TFS," "Git" or "Subversion" for improved team collaboration. Business requirements and associated tasks and functionalities are stored in an agile project tracking system like "JIRA," "Rally" and "Azure DevOps" to enable enhanced tracking of code for every single functionality. These tools also help in the estimation of resources and costs involved through the project lifecycle. To ensure effective management of each project, information security and team collaboration, TDSP confers the creation of separate storage for each project on the version control system. The adoption of a standardized structure for all the projects within an organization aid in the creation of an institutional knowledge library across the organization.

The TDSP lifecycle provides standard templates for all the required documents as well as folder structure at a centralized location. The files containing programming codes for the data exploration and extraction of the functionality can be organized to using the provided a folder structure, which also holds records pertaining to model iterations. These templates allow the team members to easily understand the work that has been completed by others as well as for a seamless addition of new team members to a given project. The markdown format supports ease of accessibility as well as making edits or updates to the document templates. To make sure the project goal and objectives are well defined and also to ensure the expected quality of the deliverables, these templates provide various checklists with important questions for each project. For example, a "project charter" can be used to document the project scope and the business problem that is being resolved by the project; standardized data reports are used to document the "structure and statistics" of the data.

Infrastructure and Resources for Data Science Projects

To effectively store infrastructure and manage shared analytics, the TDSP recommends using tools like: "machine learning service," databases, "big data clusters," and cloud based systems to store data sets. The analytics and storage infrastructure that houses raw as well as processed or cleaned data sets can be cloud-based or on-premises. D analytics and storage infrastructure permits the reproducibility of analysis and prevents duplication and the redundancy of data that can created inconsistency and unwarranted infrastructure costs. Tools are supplied to grant specific permissions to the shared resources and to track their activity, which in turn allows secure access to the resources for each member of the team.

Tools and Utilities for Project Execution

The introduction of any changes to an existing process tends to be rather challenging in most organizations. To encourage and raise the consistency of adoption of these changes, several tools can be implemented that are provided by the TDSP. Some of the basic tasks in the data science lifecycle including "data exploration" and "baseline modeling" can be easily automated with the tools provided by TDSP. To allow hassle free contribution of shared tools and utilities into the team's "shared code repository," TDSP from provides a well defined structure. This results in cost savings by allowing other project teams within the organization to reuse and repurpose these shared tools and utilities.

The TDSP lifecycle serves as a standardized template with a well-defined set of artifacts that can be used to garner effective team collaboration and communication across the board. This lifecycle is comprised of a selection of the best practices and structures from "Microsoft" to facilitated successful delivery predictive analytics Solutions and intelligent applications.

Let's look at the details of each of the five stages of the TDSP lifecycle, namely, "Business understanding," "Data acquisition in understanding," "modeling," "deployment" and "customer acceptance."

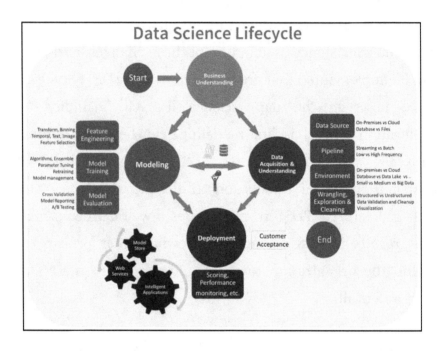

Stage I – Business Understanding

The goal of this stage is to gather and drill down on the essential variables that will be used as targets for the model, and the metrics associated with these variables will ultimately determine the overall success of the project. Another significant objective of this stage is the identification of required data sources that the company already has or may need to procure. At this stage, the two primary tasks that are required to be accomplished are: "defining objects and identifying data sources."

Defining objectives

All projects must always start with the identification of the key business variables that the analytical tools are required to predict. These variables are called "model targets," and the metrics associated with these model targets, such as sales forecast and prediction of fraudulent orders, are used as a measure of the success of the project. To define the project goals and objectives, it is imperative to work with the stakeholders and the end users and asking relevant questions that can be highly specific or even vague. To answer these questions, the data science approach employs names and numbers. The five types of questions that are primarily used for data science or machine learning are pertaining to: "regression (how much or how many?), classification (what categories?), clustering (which groups?), anomaly detection (is this unusual?), recommendation (which option should be taken?)". It is important to determine the right questions for your project and understand how the answers to these questions will help you accomplish the business or project goals.

Specification and alignment of the roles and responsibilities of each member within the project team is quintessential to the success of the project. This can be accomplished with the help of a high level project plan containing significant milestones that can be modified as needed to the course of the project. Another important definition that should be agreed upon at this stage of the project is that all of the key performance indicators and metrics. For example, a project for prediction of customer turnover rate requiring the accuracy rate of "ABC" percent by the completion of the project can help you understand the requirement that must be fulfilled to meet the success criteria of the project. So in order to achieve the "ABC" percent accuracy rate, the company may run discount offers and promotions. The industry wide standard used in the development of metrics is called "SMART," which stands for "Specific, Measurable, Achievable, Relevant, Time bound."

Identification of data sources

The data sources that may contain "known examples" of answers to the five types of questions raised during the defining phase must be identified and accounted for. You must look for data that is in direct relevance to the questions asked and assess if you have a measurable target and features related to those targets. The data that serves as an accurate measure for the model target and its features is crucial for the determination of the project's success. For example, you might encounter a situation where the existing system is unable to collect and record the types of data that are required to accomplish the project goals. This should immediately inform you that you need to start looking for external data sources or run a system update to enable the collection of additional data types by the existing system.

Deliverables to be created in this stage

- **Charter document** – It is a "living document" that needs to be updated throughout the course of the project, in light of new project discoveries and changing business requirements. A standard template is supplied with the TDSP "project structure definition." It is important to build upon this document by adding more details throughout the course of the project while keeping the stakeholders promptly updated on all changes made.

- **Data sources** – Within the TDSP "project data report folder," the data sources can be found within the "Raw Data Sources" section of the "Data Definitions Report." The "Raw Data Sources" section also specifies the initial and final locations of the raw data and provide additional details like the "coding scripts" to move up the data to any desired environment.

- **Data dictionaries** – The descriptions of the characteristics and features of the data such as the "data schematics" and available "entity relationship diagrams," provided by the stakeholders are documented within the Data dictionaries.

Stage II – Data Acquisition and Understanding

The goal of this stage is the production of high quality processed data set with defined relationships to the model targets and location of the data set in the required analytics environment. At this stage, the "solution architecture" of the data pipeline must also be developed, which will allow regular updates to and scoring of the data. The three primary tasks that must be completed during this stage are: "Data ingestion, Data exploration and Data pipeline set up."

Data ingestion

The process required to transfer the data from the source location to the target location should be set up in this phase. The target locations are determined by the environments that will allow you to perform analytical activities like training and predictions.

Data exploration

The data set must be scrubbed to remove any discrepancies and errors before it can be used to train the Data models. To check the data quality and gathered information required to process the data before modeling, tools such as data summarization and visualization should be used. Since this process is repeated multiple times, an automated utility called "IDEAR," which is provided by TDSP can be used for Data visualization and creation of Data summary reports. With the achievement of satisfactory quality of the processed data, the inherent data patterns can be observed. This, in turn, helps in the selection and development of an appropriate "predictive model" for the target. Now you must assess if you have the required amount of data to start the modeling process, which is iterative in nature and may require you to identify new data sources to achieve higher relevance and accuracy.

Set up a data pipeline

To supplement the iterative process of data modeling, a standard process for scoring new data and refreshing the existing data set must be established by setting up a "data pipeline or workflow." The solution architecture of the data pipeline must be developed by the end of this stage. There are three types of pipelines that can be used on the basis of the business needs and constraints of the existing system: "batch based," "real-time or streaming," and "hybrid."

Deliverables to be created in this stage

- **Data quality report** – This report must include a "data summary" relationship between the business requirement and its attributes and variable ranking among other details. The "IDEAR" tool supplied with TDSP it's capable of generating data quality reports on a relational table, CSV file, or any other tabular data set.

- **Solution architecture** – A description or a diagram of the data pipeline that is used to score new data and generated predictions, after the model has been built can be referred to as "solution architecture." This diagram can also provide the data pipeline needed to "retrain" the model based on new data.

- **Checkpoint decision** –Prior to that start of the actual model building process project must be reevaluated to determine if the expected value can be achieved by pursuing the project. These are also called "Go or No-Go" decisions.

Stage III – Modeling

The goal of this stage is to find "optimal data features" for the machine learning model, which is informative enough to predict the target variables accurately and can be deployed in the production environment. The three primary tasks that must be accomplished in this stage are: "feature engineering, model training, and the determination of the suitability of the model for the production environment."

Feature engineering

The data features must be created from the raw data variables using the process of "inclusion, aggregation, and transformation." To be able to understand the functioning of the model, a clear understanding of how these data features relate to one another as well as to the machine learning algorithms that will be using those features must be developed. The insights gathered from the data exploration phase can be combined with domain expertise to allow creative feature engineering. The fine act of determining and including informative variables while making sure a whole lot of unrelated variables are not included in the data set is referred to as feature engineering. Too many unrelated variables will add noise to the data model, so an attempt must be made to add as many informative variables as possible to get better results. The features must also be generated for any new data collected doing the scoring.

Model training

A wide variety of modeling algorithms are available in the market today. The algorithm that meets the criteria of your project must be selected. The process for "model training" can be divided into four steps which are:

1. Creation of a "training data set" as well as a "test data set" by appropriately dividing the input data.
2. Development of the model with the use of the "training data set."
3. Evaluation of the training and the test data set, by employing various machine learning algorithms as well as related "tuning parameters" that are designed to help answer the previously discussed five types of questions from the existing data set.
4. Assess the best fit for the solution to resolve the business problem by comparing all available methods using key performance indicators and metrics.

TDSP provides an "automated modeling and reporting tool" that is capable of running through multiple algorithms and "parameters sweeps" to develop a "baseline model" as well as a "baseline modeling report" that can serve as a performance summary for each "model and parameter combination."

Deliverables to be created in this stage

- **Feature sets** – The document containing all the features described in the "feature sets section of the data definition report." It is heavily used by the programmers to write the required code and develop features based on the basis of the description provided by the document.
- **Model report** – This document must contain the details of each model that was evaluated based on a standard template report.
- **Checkpoint decisions** – A decision regarding deployment of the model to the production environment must be made on the basis of the performance of different models.

Stage IV – Deployment

The goal of this stage is to release the solution models to a lower production like environments such as pre-production environment and user acceptance testing environment before eventually deploying the model in the production environment. The primary task to be accomplished in this stage is "operationalization of the model."

Operationalize the model

Once you have obtained a set of models with expected performance levels, these models can then be operationalized for other applicable applications to use. According to the business requirements, predictions can be made in real-time or on a batch basis. In order to deploy the model, they must be integrated with an open "Application Programming Interface" (API) to allow interaction of the model with all other applications and its components, as needed.

Deliverables to be created in this stage

- A dashboard report using the key performance indicators and metrics to access the health of the system.
- A document or run book with the details of the deployment plan for the final model.
- A document containing the solution architecture of the final model.

Stage V – Customer Acceptance

The goal of this stage is to ensure that the final solution for the project meets the expectations of the stakeholders and fulfills the business requirements gathered during Stage I of the Data science lifecycle. The two primary tasks that must be accomplished in this stage are: "system validation and project hand-off."

System validation – The final solution that will be deployed in the production environment must be evaluated against the business requirements and the data pipeline to make sure that the stakeholders needs are met. The stakeholder must validate that the system meets their business needs and resolves the problem that started the project in the first place. All the documentation must be thoroughly reviewed and finalized by the end of this stage.

Project hand-off – At this stage, the project must be transferred from the development team to the post production and maintenance team. For example, IT support team or someone from the stakeholder's team dad will provide day-to-day support for the solution in the production environment.

Deliverables to be created in this stage

The most important document created during this stage is for the stakeholders and called an "exit report." The document contains all of the available details of the project that are significant to provide an understanding of the operations of the system. TDSP supplies a standardized template for the "exit report," that can be easily customized to cater to specific stakeholder needs.

Types of Data

Now that you understand the importance of data science let us look at different types of data so you can choose the most appropriate analytical tools and algorithms is on the type of data that needs to be processed. Data types can be divided into two at a very high level: qualitative and quantitative.

Qualitative data – Any data that cannot be measured and only observed subjectively by adding a qualitative feature to the object it's called as "qualitative data." Classification of an object using unmeasurable features results in the creation of qualitative data. For example, attributes like color, smell, texture and taste. There are three types of qualitative data:

"Binary or binomial data" – Data values that signal mutually exclusive events where only one of the two categories or options is correct and applicable. For example, true or false, yes or no, positive or negative. Consider a box of assorted tea bags. You try all the different flavors and group the ones that you like as "good" and the ones you don't as "bad." In this case, "good or bad" would be categorized as binomial data type. This type of data is widely used in the development of statistical models for predictive analysis.

"Nominal or unordered data" – Data characteristics that lack an "implicit or natural value" can be referred to as nominal data. Consider a box of M&Ms, you can record the color of each M&M in the box in a worksheet, and that would serve as nominal data. This kind of data is widely used to assess statistical differences in the data set, using techniques like "Chi Square analysis," which could tell you "statistically significant differences" in the amount of each color of M&M in a box.

"Ordered or ordinal data" – The characteristics of this Data type do have certain "implicit or natural of value" such as small, medium, or large. For example, online reviews on the sites like "Yelp," "Amazon," and "Trip Advisor" have a rating scale from 1 to 5, implying 5 star rating is better than 4, which is better than 3 and so on.

Quantitative data – Any characteristics of the data that can be measured objectively are called as "quantitative data." Classification of an object in using measurable features and giving it a numerical value results and creation of quantitative data. For example, product prices, temperature, dimensions like length etc. There are two types of quantitative data:

"Continuous Data" – Data values that can be defined to a further lower level, such as units of measurement like kilometers, meters, centimeters, and on and on, are called as continuous data type. For example, you can purchase a bag of almonds by weight like 500 g or 8 ounces. This accounts for continuous data type, which is primarily used to test and verify different kinds of hypotheses such as assessing the accuracy of the weight printed on the bag of almonds.

"Discrete Data" – numerical data value that cannot be divided and reduced to a higher level of precision, such as the number of cars owned by a person which can only be accounted for as indivisible numbers (you cannot have 1.5 or 2.3 cars), is called as discrete data types. For example, you can purchase another bag of ice cream bars by the number of ice cream bars inside the package, like four or six. This accounts for the discrete data type, which can be used in combination with continuous data type to perform a regression analysis to verify if the total weight of the ice cream box (continuous data) is correlated with the number of ice cream bars (discrete data) inside.

Data Science Strategies

Data science is mainly used in decision-making by making

precise predictions with the use of "predictive causal analytics," "prescriptive analytics," and machine learning.

Predictive causal analytics – The "predictive causal analytics" can be applied to develop a model that can accurately predict and forecast the likelihood of a particular event occurring in the future. For example, financial institutions use predictive causal analytics based tools to assess the likelihood of a customer defaulting on their credit card payments, by generating a model that can analyze the payment history of the customer with all of their borrowing institutions.

Prescriptive analytics - The "prescriptive analytics" are widely used in the development of "intelligent tools and applications" that are capable of modifying and learning with dynamic parameters and make their own "decisions." The tool not only predicts the occurrence of a future event but is also capable of providing recommendations on a variety of actions and its resulting outcomes. For example, the self-driving cars gather driving related data with every driving experience and use it to train themselves to make better driving and maneuvering decisions.

Machine learning to make predictions – To develop models that can determine future trends based on the transactional data acquired by the company, machine learning algorithms are a necessity. This is considered as "supervised machine learning," which we will elaborate on later in this book. For example, fraud detection systems use machine learning algorithms on the historical data pertaining to fraudulent purchases to detect if a transaction is fraudulent.

Machine learning for pattern discovery – To be able to develop models that are capable of identifying hidden data patterns but lack required parameters to make future predictions, the "unsupervised machine learning algorithms," such as "Clustering," need to be employed. For example, telecom companies often use the "clustering" technology to expand their network by identifying network tower locations with optimal signal strength in the targeted region.

Data Science vs Data Analysis

The terms of data science and data analytics are often used interchangeably. However, these terms are completely different and have different implications for different businesses. Data science encompasses a variety of scientific models and methods that can be used to manipulate and analyze structured, semi structured, and unstructured data. Tools and processes that can be used to make sense of gather insight from highly complex, unorganized and raw data set falls under the umbrella of data science. Unlike data analytics that is targeted to verify a hypothesis, data science boils down to connecting data points to identify new patterns and insights that can be made use of in future planning for the business. Data science moves the business from inquiry to insights by providing a new perspective into their structured and unstructured data by identifying patterns that can allow businesses to increase efficiencies, reduce costs and recognize the new market opportunities.

Data science acts as a multidisciplinary blend of technology, machine learning algorithm development, statistical analysis, and data inference that provides businesses with enhanced capability to solve their most complex business problems. Data analytics falls under the umbrella of data science and pertains more to reviewing and analyzing historical data to put it in context. Unlike data science, data analytics is characterized by low usage of artificial intelligence, predictive modeling and machine learning algorithms to gather insights from processed and structured data using standard SQL query commands. The seemingly nuanced differences between data analytics and data science can actually have a substantial impact on an organization.

Data Science in Cyber Security

The ability to analyze and closely examine Data trends and patterns using Machine learning algorithms has resulted in the significant application of data science in the cyber security space. With the use of data science, companies are not only able to identify the specific network terminal(s) that initiated the cyber-attack but are also in a position to predict potential future attacks on their systems and take required measures to prevent the attacks from happening in the first place. Use of "active intrusion detection systems" that are capable of monitoring users and devices on any network of choice and flag any unusual activity serves as a powerful weapon against hackers and cyber attackers. While the "predictive intrusion detection systems" that are capable of using machine learning algorithms on historical data to detect potential security threats serves as a powerful shield against the cyber predators.

Cyber-attacks can result in a loss of priceless data and information resulting in extreme damage to the organization. To secure and protect the data set, sophisticated encryption and complex signatures can be used to prevent unauthorized access. Data science can help with the development of such impenetrable protocols and algorithms. By analyzing the trends and patterns of previous cyber-attacks on companies across different industrial sectors, Data science can help detect the most frequently targeted data set and even predict potential future cyber-attacks. Companies rely heavily on the data generated and authorized by their customers but in the light of increasing cyber-attacks, customers are extremely wary of their personal information being compromised and are looking to take their businesses to the companies that are able to assure them of their data security and privacy by implementing advanced data security tools and technologies. This is where data science is becoming the saving grace of the companies by helping them enhance their cyber security measures.

Chapter 2: Introduction to Python Coding

Python was first implemented in 1989 and is regarded as highly user-friendly and simple to learn programming language for entry level coders and amateurs. It is a high-level programming language, commonly used for general purposes. It was originally developed by Guido van Rossum at the "Center Wiskunde & Informatica (CWI), Netherlands," in the 1980s and introduced by the "Python Software Foundation" in 1991. It was designed primarily to emphasize the readability of programming code, and its syntax enables programmers to convey ideas using fewer lines of code. Python programming language increases the speed of operation while allowing for higher efficiency in creating system integrations. It is regarded as ideal for individuals newly interested in programming or coding and needs to comprehend programming fundamentals. This stems from the fact that Python reads almost the same as English language. Therefore, it requires less time to understand how the language works and focus can be directed in learning the basics of programming.

Python is an interpreted language that supports automatic memory management and object-oriented programming. This extremely intuitive and flexible programming language can be used for coding projects such as machine learning algorithms, web applications, data mining and visualization, game development.

Installation Instructions for Python

Follow the s instructions below to download and install Python on your operating system by referring to the relevant section. The latest version of Python released in the middle of 2019 is Python 3.8.0. Make sure to download and install the most recent and stable version of Python at the time.

WINDOWS

1. From the official Python website, click on the "Downloads" icon and select Windows.
2. Click on the "Download Python 3.8.0" button to view all the downloadable files.
3. On subsequent screen, select the Python version you would like to download. In this book, we will be using the Python 3 version under "Stable Releases." So scroll down the page and click on the "Download Windows x86-64 executable installer" link, as shown in the picture below.

- Python 3.8.0 - Oct. 14, 2019

  Note that Python 3.8.0 *cannot* be used on Windows XP or earlier.

  - Download Windows help file
  - Download Windows x86-64 embeddable zip file
  - Download Windows x86-64 executable installer
  - Download Windows x86-64 web-based installer
  - Download Windows x86 embeddable zip file
  - Download Windows x86 executable installer
  - Download Windows x86 web-based installer

4. A pop up window titled "python-3.8.0-amd64.exe" will be shown.

5. Click on the "Save File" button to start downloading the file.

6. Once the download has completed, double click the saved file icon, and a "Python 3.8.0 (64-bit) Setup" pop window will be shown.

7. Make sure that you select the "Install Launcher for all users (recommended)" and the "Add Python 3.8 to PATH" checkboxes. Note – If you already have an older version of Python installed on your system, the "Upgrade Now" button will appear instead of the "Install Now" button, and neither of the checkboxes will be shown.

8. Click on "Install Now" and a "User Account Control" pop up window will be shown.

9. A notification stating, "Do you want to allow this app to make changes to your device" will be shown, click on Yes.

10. A new pop up window titled "Python 3.8.0 (64-bit) Setup" will be shown containing a setup progress bar.

11. Once the installation has been completed, a "Set was successful" message will be shown. Click on Close.

12. To verify the installation, navigate to the directory where you installed Python and double click on the python.exe file.

MACINTOSH

1. From the official Python website, click on the "Downloads" icon and select Mac.

2. Click on the "Download Python 3.8.0" button to view all the downloadable files.

3. On the subsequent screen, select the Python version you would like to download. In this book, we will be using the Python 3 version under "Stable Releases." So scroll down the page and click on the "Download macOS 64-bit installer" link under Python 3.8.0, as shown in the picture below.

- Python 3.7.5 · Oct. 15, 2019
  - Download macOS 64-bit/32-bit installer
  - Download macOS 64-bit installer
- Python 3.8.0 · Oct. 14, 2019
  - Download macOS 64-bit installer
- Python 3.7.4 · July 8, 2019
  - Download macOS 64-bit/32-bit installer
  - Download macOS 64-bit installer
- Python 3.6.9 · July 2, 2019

4. A pop up window titled "python-3.8.0-macosx10.9.pkg" will be shown.

5. Click "Save File" to start downloading the file.

6. Once the download has completed, double click the saved file icon, and an "Install Python" pop window will be shown.

7. Click "Continue" to proceed, and the terms and conditions pop up window will appear.

8. Click Agree and then click "Install."

9. A notification requesting administrator permission and password will be shown. Enter your system password to start installation.

10. Once the installation has finished, an "Installation was successful" message will appear. Click on the Close button, and you are all set.

11. To verify the installation, navigate to the directory where you installed Python and double click on the python launcher icon that will take you to the Python Terminal.

LINUX

- **For Red Hat, CentOS, or Fedora,** install the python3 and python3-devel packages.

- **For Debian or Ubuntu,** install the python3.x and python3.x-dev packages.

- **For Gentoo,** install the '=python-3.x*' ebuild (you may have to unmask it first).

1. From the official Python website, click on the "Downloads" icon and select Linux/UNIX.

2. Click on the "Download Python 3.8.0" button to view all the downloadable files.

3. On subsequent screen, select the Python version you would like to download. In this book, we will be using the Python 3 version under "Stable Releases." So scroll down the page and click on the "Download Gzipped source tarball" link under Python 3.8.0, as shown in the picture below.

- Download Gzipped source tarball
- Download XZ compressed source tarball
  - Python 3.8.0 - Oct. 14, 2019
    - Download Gzipped source tarball
    - Download XZ compressed source tarball
  - Python 3.7.4 - July 8, 2019
    - Download Gzipped source tarball
    - Download XZ compressed source tarball

4. A pop up window titled "python-3.7.5.tgz" will be shown.

5. Click "Save File" to begin downloading the file.

6. Once the download has finished, double click the saved file icon, and an "Install Python" pop window will appear.

7. Follow the prompts on the screen to complete the installation process.

Getting Started

With the Python terminal installed on your computer, you can now start writing and executing the Python code. All Python codes are written in a text editor as (.py) files and executed on the Python interpreter command line as shown in the code below, where "nineplanets.py" is the name of the Python file:

"C: \Users\Your Name\python nineplanets.py"

You will be able to test a small code without writing it in a file and simply executing it as a command line itself by typing the

169

code below on the Mac, Windows or Linux command line, as shown below:

"C: \Users\Your Name\python"

In case the command above does not work, use the code below instead:

"C: \Users\Your Name\py"

Indentation – The importance of indentation, which is the number of spaces preceding the code, is fundamental to the Python coding structure. In most programming languages, indentation is added to enhance the readability of the code. However, in Python, the indentation is used to indicate execution of a subset of the code, as shown in the code below

If 7 > 2:
    print ('Seven is greater than two')

Indentation precedes the second line of code with the print command. If the indentation is skipped and the code was written as below, an error will be triggered:

If 7 > 2:
print ('Seven is greater than two')

The number of spaces can be modified but is required to have at least one space. For example, you can execute the code below with higher indentation, but for a specific set of code same number of spaces must be used, or you will receive an error.

If 7 > 2:
    print ('Seven is greater than two')

Adding Comments – In Python, comments can be added to the code by starting the code comment lines with a "#," as shown in the example below:

#Any relevant comments will be added here
print ('Nine planets')

Comments serve as a description of the code and will not be executed by the Python terminal. Make sure to remember that any comments at the end of the code line will lead to the entire code line being skipped by the Python terminal, as shown in the code below. Comments can be very useful in case you need to stop the execution when you are testing the code.

print ('Nine Planets')   #Comments added here

Multiple lines of comments can be added by starting each code line with "#," as shown below:

#Comments added here
#Supplementing the comments here
#Further adding the comments here
print ('Nine Planets')

Python Variables

In Python, variables are primarily utilized to save data values without executing a command for it. A variable can be created by simply assigning the desired value to it, as shown in the example below:

A = 999
B = 'Patricia'
print (A)
print (B)

A variable could be declared without a specific data type. The data type of a variable can also be modified after it's an initial declaration, as shown in the example below:

A = 999 # A has data type set as int
A = 'Patricia' # A now has data type str
print (A)

Some of the rules applied to the Python variable names are as follows:

1. Variable names could be as short as single alphabets or more descriptive words like height, weight, and more.
2. Variable names could only be started with an underscore character or a letter.
3. Variable names must not start with numbers.
4. Variable names can contain underscores or alpha numeric characters. No other special characters are allowed.
5. Variable names are case sensitive. For example, 'weight,' 'Weight,' and 'WEIGHT' will be accounted as 3 separate variables.

Assigning Value to Variables

In Python, multiple variables can be assigned DISTINCT values in a single code line, as shown in the example below:

A, B, C = 'violet,' maroon, 'teal'
print (A)
print (B)
print (C)

OR multiple variables can be assigned SAME value in a single code line, as shown in the example below:

```
A, B, C = 'violet'
print (A)
print (B)
print (C)
```

Python Data Types

Python supports a variety of data types, as listed below. To build a solid understanding of the concept of variables, you must learn all the Python data types.

Category	Data Type	Example Syntax
Text	*"str"*	'Nine Planets' "Nine Planets" """"Nine Planets""""
Boolean	*"bool"*	'True' 'False'
Mapping (mixed data types, associative array of key and value pairs)	*"dict"*	'{'key8' : 8.0, 5 : True}'
Sequence (may contain mixed data types)	*"list"*	'[8.0, 'character', True]'
	"tuple"	'[8.0, 'character', True]'
	"range"	'range (11, 51)' 'range (110, 51, 11, -11, -51, -110)'
Binary	*"bytes"*	b 'byte sequences' b 'byte sequences' bytes ([121, 91, 75, 110])
	"bytearray"	bytearray (b 'byte sequences') bytearray (b 'byte sequences') bytearray ([121, 91. 75,

		110])
	"memoryview"	
Set (unordered, no duplicates, mixed data types)	*"set"*	'[8.0, 'character', True]'
	"frozenset"	'frozenset ([8.0, 'character', True])'
Numeric	*"int"*	'35'
	"float"	'155e3'
	"complex"	'155 + 2.1j'
Ellipsis (index in NumPy arrays)	*"ellipsis"*	'...' 'Ellipsis'

To view the data type of any object, you can use the *"type ()"* function as shown in the example below:

A = 'Violet'
print (type (A))

Assigning the Data Type to Variables

A new variable can be created by simply declaring a value for it. This set data value will in turn assign the data type to the variable.

To assign a specific data type to a variable, the constructor functions listed below are used:

Constructor Functions	**Data Type**
A = str ('Nine Planets)'	str
A = int (55)	Int (Must be a whole number, positive or negative with no decimals, no length restrictions)

A = float (14e6)	Float (Floating point number must be positive or negative number with one or more decimals; maybe scientific number an 'e' to specify an exponential power of 10)
A = complex (92j)	Complex (Must be written with a 'j' as an imaginary character)
A = list (('teal', maroon, 'jade'))	list
A = range (3, 110)	range
A = tuple (('teal', maroon, 'jade'))	tuple
A = set (('teal', maroon, 'jade'))	set
A = frozenset (('teal', 'jade', maroon))	frozenset
A = dict ('color' : maroon, 'year' : 1988)	dict
A = bool (False)	bool
A = bytes (542)	bytes
A = bytearray (9)	bytearray
A = memoryview (bytes (525))	memoryview

EXERCISE – To solidify your understanding of data types. Look at the first column of the table below and write the data type for that variable. Once you have all your answers, look at the second column, and verify your answers.

Variable	Data Type
A = 'Nine Planets'	str
A = 45	int
A = 56e2	float
A = 34j	complex

A = ['teal', maroon, 'jade']	list
A = range (12, 103)	range
A = ('teal', maroon, 'jade')	tuple
A = {'teal', maroon, 'jade'}	set
A = frozenset ({ 'teal', 'jade', maroon})	frozenset
A = ['color' : maroon, 'year' : 1939}	dict
A = False	bool
A = b 'Morning'	bytes
A = bytearray (5)	bytearray
A = memoryview (bytes (45))	memoryview

Output Variables

In order to retrieve variables as output, the "print" statements are used in Python. You can use the "+" character to combine text with a variable for final output, as shown in the example below:

'A = maroon
print ('Flowers are' + A)'

OUTPUT – 'Flowers are maroon'

A variable can also be combined with another variable using the "+" character as shown in the example below:

'A = 'Flowers are'
B = maroon
AB = A + B
print (AB)'

OUTPUT – 'Flowers are maroon'

However, when the "+" character is used with numeric values, it retains its function as mathematical operator, as shown in the example below:

'A = 22
B = 33
print (A + B)'

OUTPUT = 55

You will not be able to combine a string of characters with numbers and will trigger an error instead, as shown in the example below:

A = yellow
B = 30
print (A + B)

OUTPUT – N/A – ERROR

Python Numbers

In Python programming, you will be working with 3 different numeric data types, namely, "int", "float" and "complex". In the previous chapter, you learned the details of what these data types entail, but below are some examples to refresh your memory.

Data Type	Example
Int (Must be a whole number, positive or negative	388 or 3.42

with no decimals, no length restrictions)	
Float (Floating point number must be a positive or negative number with one or more decimals; maybe scientific number an "e" to specify an exponential power of 10)	41e4
Complex (Must be written with a "j" as an imaginary character)	46j

EXERCISE – Create variable "a" with data value as "4.25", variable "b" with data value as "7e3" and variable "c" with data value as "-59j".

USE YOUR DISCRETION HERE AND WRITE YOUR CODE FIRST

Now, check your code against the correct code below:

```
a = 4.25      # int
b = 7e3       # float
c = -59j      # complex


print (type (a))
print (type (b))
print (type (c))
```

Note – The # comments are not required for the correct code and are only mentioned to bolster your understanding of the concept.

Converting one numeric data type to another

As all Python variables are dynamic in nature, you will be able to convert the data type of these variables if needed by deriving a new variable from the variable that you would like to assign a new data type.

Let's continue building on the exercise discussed above.

```
a = 4.25      # int
b = 7e3       # float
c = -49j      # complex
```

```
#conversion from int to float
x = float (a)
```

```
#conversion from float to complex
y = complex (b)
```

```
#conversion from complex to int
z = float (c)
```

```
#conversion from int to complex
x1 = int (a)

print (x)
print (y)
print (z)
print (x1)


print (type (x))
print (type (y))
print (type (z))
print (type (x1))
```

EXERCISE – View a random number between 11 and 21 by importing the random module.

USE YOUR DISCRETION HERE AND WRITE YOUR CODE FIRST

Now, check your code against the correct code below:

```
import random

print (random.randrange (11, 21))
```

Variable Casting with Constructor Functions

In the discussion and exercise above, you learned that variables can be declared by simply assigning desired data value to them and thereby, the variables will assume the pertinent data type based on the data value. However, Python allows you to specify the data types for variables by using classes or "constructor functions" to define the data type for variables. This process is called "Casting."

Here are the 3 constructor functions used for "casting" numeric data type to a variable.

Constructor Functions	Data Type
int ()	Will construct an integer number from an integer literal, a string literal (provided the string is representing a whole number) or a float literal (by rounding down to the preceding whole number)
float ()	Will construct a float number from a string literal (provided the string is

	representing a float or an integer), a float literal or an integer literal
complex ()	Will construct a string from a large number of data types, such as integer literals, float literals, and strings

Here are some examples:

Integer:

a = int (7)   # a takes the value 7
b = int (2.8)   # b takes the value 3
c = int ('6')   # c takes the value 6

Float:

a = float (7)   # a takes the value 7.0
b = float (2.8)   # b takes the value 2.8
c – float ('6')   # c takes the value 6.0

String:

a = str ('serial')   # a takes the value 'serial'
b = str (2.8)   # b takes the value '2.8'
c = str ('6')   # c takes the value '6.0'

Python Strings

In Python, string data type for a variable is denoted by using single, double, or triple quotation marks. This implies that you can assign string data value to variable by quoting the string of characters. For example, "welcome" is the same as 'welcome' and "'welcome'".

EXERCISE – Create a variable "v" with a string data value as "I like teal" and display it.

USE YOUR DISCRETION HERE AND WRITE YOUR CODE FIRST

Now, check your code against the correct code below:

v = 'I like teal'
print (v)

OUTPUT – I like teal

EXERCISE – Create a variable "A" with a multiple line string data value as "Looking at the sky tonight, thinking of you by my side!

Let the world go on and on; it will be alright if I stay strong!" and display it.

USE YOUR DISCRETION HERE AND WRITE YOUR CODE FIRST

Now, check your code against the correct code below:

a = """Looking at the sky tonight,
thinking of you by my side!
Let the world go on and on,
it will be alright if I stay strong!"""
print (a)

OUTPUT – Looking at the sky tonight,
thinking of you by my side!
Let the world go on and on,
it will be alright if I stay strong!

Note – You must use triple quote to create multiline string data values.

String Arrays

In Python, string data values are arrays of bytes that represent Unicode characters as true for most programming languages. But unlike other programming languages, Python lacks data type for individual characters, which are denoted as string data type with length of 1.

The first character of every string is given the position of 'o', and subsequently, the subsequent characters will have the position as 1, 2, 3, and so on. In order to display desired characters from a string data value, you can use the position of the character enclosed in square brackets. For example, if you wanted to display the fourth character of the string data value "cranberry" of variable "x." You will use the command "print (x [3])"

EXERCISE – Create a variable "P" with a string data value as "wonderful" and display the fifth character of this string.

USE YOUR DISCRETION HERE AND WRITE YOUR CODE FIRST

Now, check your code against the correct code below:

P = 'wonderful'
print (P [4])

OUTPUT – e

Slicing

If you would like to view a range of characters, you can do so by specifying the start and the end index of the desired positions and separating the indexes by a colon. For example, to view characters of a string from position 2 to position 5, your code will be *"print (variable [2:5])"*.

You can even view the characters starting from the end of the string by using "negative indexes" and start slicing the string from the end of the string. For example, to view characters of a string from position 3 to position 1, your code will be *"print (variable [-3 : -2])"*.

In order to view the length of the string, you can use the "len ()" function. For example, to view the length of a string, your code will be *"print (len (variable))."*

EXERCISE – Create a variable "P" with a string data value as "birds can sing!" and display characters from position 2 to 5 of this string.

USE YOUR DISCRETION HERE AND WRITE YOUR CODE FIRST*

Now, check your code against the correct code below:

```
P = 'birds can sing!'
print (P [2 : 5])
```

OUTPUT – rdsc

EXERCISE – Create a variable "x" with a string data value as "coding is easy" and display characters from position 4 to 1, starting the count from the end of this string.

USE YOUR DISCRETION HERE AND WRITE YOUR CODE FIRST*

Now, check your code against the correct code below:

```
x = 'coding is easy'
print (x [-4 : -2])
```

OUTPUT - ea

EXERCISE – Create a variable "z" with a string data value as "good morning" and display the length of this string.

USE YOUR DISCRETION HERE AND WRITE YOUR CODE FIRST

Now, check your code against the correct code below:

z = 'good morning'
print (len (z))

OUTPUT - 11

String Methods

There are various built-in methods in Python that can be applied to string data values. Here are the Python codes for some of the most frequently used string methods, using variable *"P = 'birds can sing!'"*.

"strip ()" method – To remove any blank spaces at the start and the end of the string.

P = " birds can sing! "
print (P.strip ())

OUTPUT – birds can sing!

"lower ()" method – To result in all the characters of a string in lower case.

P = "Birds can sing!"
print (P.lower ())

OUTPUT – birds can sing!

"upper ()" method – To result in all the characters of a string in upper case.

P = "Birds can sing!"
print (P.upper ())

OUTPUT – BIRDS CAN SING!
"replace ()" method – To replace select characters of a string.

P = "birds can sing!"
print (P.replace ("birds", "Songbirds"))

OUTPUT – Songbirds can sing!

"split ()" method – To split a string into substrings using comma as the separator.

P = "Birds, Songbirds"
print (P.split (","))

OUTPUT – ['Birds', 'Songbirds']

String Concatenation

There might be instances when you need to collate different string variables. This can be accomplished with the use of the "+" logical operator. Here's the syntax for this Python code:

X = "string1"
Y = "string2"
Z = X + Y
print (Z)

Similarly, below is the syntax to insert a blank space between two different string variables.

X = "string1"
Y = "string2"
Z = X + " " + Y

print (Z)

However, Python does not permit concatenation of string variables with numeric variables. But can be accomplished with the use of the *"format ()"* method, which will format the executed arguments and place them in the string where the placeholders "{ }" are used. Here's the syntax for this Python code:

X = numeric
Y = "String"
print (Y. format (X))

EXERCISE – Create two variables "A" and "B" with string data values as "The winter" and "is coming!" and display them as a concatenated string.

USE YOUR DISCRETION HERE AND WRITE YOUR CODE FIRST

Now, check your code against the correct code below:

A = "The winter"
B = "is coming!"
C = A + B

print (C)

OUTPUT – The winter is coming!

EXERCISE – Create two variables "A" with string data values as "her lucky number is" and "B" with numeric data value as "3333" and display them as a concatenated string.

USE YOUR DISCRETION HERE AND WRITE YOUR CODE FIRST*

Now, check your code against the correct code below:

A = "her lucky number is"
B = "3333"
print (A. format (B))

OUTPUT – her lucky number is 3333

Python Booleans

In the process of developing a software program, there is often a need to confirm and verify whether an expression is true or false. This is where Python Boolean data type and data values are used. In Python, comparison and evaluation of two data values will result in one of the two Boolean values: "True" or "False".

Here are some examples of comparison statement of numeric data leading to Boolean value:

print (110 > 94)

OUTPUT – True

print (110 > 94)

OUTPUT – False

print (110 > 94)

OUTPUT – False

Let's look at the *"bool ()"* function now, which allows for evaluation of numeric data as well as string data resulting in "True" or "False" Boolean values.

print (bool (93))

OUTPUT - True

print (bool ("Welcome"))

OUTPUT - True

Here are some key points to remember for Booleans:

1. If a statement has some kind of content, it would be evaluated as "True".
2. All string data values will be result ined as "True" unless the string is empty.
3. All numeric values will be result ined as "True" except "0"
4. Lists, Tuples, Set and Dictionaries will be result ined as "True", unless they are empty.
5. Mostly empty values like (), [], {}, "", False, None and 0 will be result ined as "False".
6. Any object created with the "_len_" function that result in the data value as "0" or "False" will be evaluated as "False".

In Python there are various built-in functions function that can be evaluated as Boolean, for example, the "isinstance()" function which allows you to determine the data type of an object. Therefore, in order to check if an object is integer, the code will be as below:

X = 10
print (isinstance (X, int))

EXERCISE – Create two variables "X" with string data values as "Happy New Year!" and "Y" with numeric data value as "4.55" and evaluate them.

USE YOUR DISCRETION HERE AND WRITE YOUR CODE FIRST

Now, check your code against the correct code below:

X = "Happy New Year!"
Y = 4.55

print (bool (X))
print (bool (Y))

OUTPUT –
True
True

Python Lists

In Python, Lists are collections of data types that can be changed, organized and include duplicate values. Lists are written within square brackets, as shown in the syntax below.

X = ["string1", "string2", "string3"]

print (X)

The same concept of position applies to Lists as the string data type, which dictates that the first string is considered to be at position 0. Subsequently the strings that will follow are given position 1, 2, and so on. You can selectively display desired string from a List by referencing the position of that string inside square bracket in the print command as shown below.

X = ["string1", "string2", "string3"]

print (X [2])

OUTPUT – [string3]

Similarly, the concept of **negative indexing** is also applied to Python List. Let's look at the example below:

X = ["string1", "string2", "string3"]

print (X [-2])

OUTPUT – [string2]

You will also be able to specify a **range of indexes** by indicating the start and end of a range. The result in values of such command on a Python List would be a new List containing only the indicated items. Here is an example for your reference.

X = ["string1", "string2", "string3", "string4", "string5", "string6"]
print (X [3 : 5])

OUTPUT – ["string4", "string5"]

* Remember the first item is at position 0, and the final position of the range (4) is not included.

Now, if you do not indicate the start of this range, it will default to the position 0 as shown in the example below:

X = ["string1", "string2", "string3", "string4", "string5", "string6"]
print (X [: 4])

OUTPUT – ["string1", "string2", "string3" , *"string4"*]
Similarly, if you do not indicate the end of this range it will display all the items of the List from the indicated start range to the end of the List, as shown in the example below:

X = ["string1", "string2", "string3", "string4", "string5", "string6"]
print (X [4 :])

OUTPUT – ["string5", "string6"]

You can also specify a **range of negative indexes** to Python Lists, as shown in the example below:

X = ["string1", "string2", "string3", "string4", "string5", "string6"]
print (X [-4 : -1])

OUTPUT – ["string3", "string4", "string5"]

* Remember the last item is at position -1, and the final position of this range (-1) is not included in the Output.

There might be instances when you need to **change the data value** for a Python List. This can be accomplished by referring to the index number of that item and declaring the new value. Let's look at the example below:

X = ["string1", "string2", "string3", "string4", "string5",
"string6"]
X [2] = "newstring"
print (X)

OUTPUT – ["string1", "string2", "newstring", "string4",
"string5", "string6"]

You can also determine the **length** of a Python List using the
"len()" function, as shown in the example below:

X = ["string1", "string2", "string3", "string4", "string5"]
print (len (X))

OUTPUT – 5

Python Lists can also be changed by **adding new items** to an
existing List using the built-in "append ()" method, as shown in
the example below:

X = ["string1", "string2", "string3", "string4", "string5"]
X.append ("newstring")
print (X)

OUTPUT – ["string1", "string2", "string3", "string4", *"string5"*, "newstring"]

You can also, add a new item to an existing Python List at a specific position using the built-in "insert ()" method, as shown in the example below:

X = ["string1", "string2", "string3", "string4"]
X.insert (3, "newstring")
print (X)

OUTPUT – ["string1", "string2", "string3", "newstring"]

There might be instances when you need to **copy** an existing Python List. This can be accomplished by using the built-in "copy ( )" method or the "list ( )" method, as shown in the example below:

X = ["string1", "string2", "string3", "string4", "string5", "string6"]
Y = X.copy( )
print (Y)

OUTPUT – ["string1", "string2", "string3", "string4", "string5", "string6"]

X = ["string1", "string2", "string3", "string4", "string5", "string6"]
Y = list (X)
print (Y)

OUTPUT – ["string1", "string2", "string3", "string4", "string5", "string6"]

There are multiple built-in methods to **delete items** from a Python List.

- To selectively delete a specific item, the "remove ()" method can be used.
  X = ["string1", "string2", "string3", "string4"]
  X.remove ("string2")
  print (X)

  OUTPUT - ["string1", "string3", "string4"]

- To delete a specific item from the List, the "pop ()" method can be used with the position of the value. If no index has been indicated, the last item of the index will be removed.
  X = ["string1", "string2", "string3", "string4"]

X.pop ( )
print (X)

OUTPUT - ["string1", "string2", "string3"]

- To delete a specific index from the List, the "del ()" method can be used, followed by the index within square brackets.

X = ["string1", "string2", "string3", "string4"]
del X [2]
print (X)

OUTPUT - ["string1", "string2", "string4"]

- To delete the entire List variable, the "del ()" method can be used, as shown below.

X = ["string1", "string2", "string3", "string4"]
del X

OUTPUT - .....

- To delete all the string values from the List without deleting the variable itself, the "clear ()" method can be used, as shown below.

X = ["string1", "string2", "string3", "string4"]
X.clear()

print (X)

OUTPUT – [ ]

Concatenation of Lists

You can join multiple lists with the use of the "+" logical operator or by adding all the items from one list to another using the "append ( )" method. The "extend ( )" method can be used to add a list at the end of another list. Let's look at the examples below to understand these commands.

X = ["string1", "string2", "string3", "string4"]
Y = [11, 22, 33, 40]

Z = X + Y
print (Z)

OUTPUT – ["string1", "string2", "string3", "string4", 11, 22, 33, 40]

X = ["string1", "string2", "string3", "string4"]
Y = [11, 22, 33, 40]

For x in Y:

X.append (x)

print (X)

OUTPUT – ["string1", "string2", "string3", "string4", 11, 22, 33, 40]

X = ["string1", "string2", "string3"]
Y = [11, 22, 33]

X.extend (Y)
print (X)

OUTPUT – ["string1", "string2", "string3", 11, 22, 33]

EXERCISE – Create a list "A" with string data values as "red, jade, teal, violet, yellow" and display the item at -2 position.

USE YOUR DISCRETION HERE AND WRITE YOUR CODE FIRST*

Now, check your code against the correct code below:

A = ["red," "jade," "teal," "violet," "yellow"]
print (A [-2])

OUTPUT – ["violet"]

EXERCISE – Create a list "A" with string data values as "red, jade, teal, violet, yellow" and display the items ranging from the string on the second position to the end of the string.

USE YOUR DISCRETION HERE AND WRITE YOUR CODE FIRST

Now, check your code against the correct code below:

A = ["red," "jade," "teal," "violet," "yellow"]
print (A [2 :])

OUTPUT – ["red," "teal," "teal," "violet," "yellow"]

EXERCISE – Create a list "A" with string data values as "red, jade, teal, violet, yellow" and replace the string "jade" to "teal."

USE YOUR DISCRETION HERE AND WRITE YOUR CODE FIRST

Now, check your code against the correct code below:

A = ["red," "jade," "teal," "violet," "yellow"]

206

A [1] = ["teal"]

print (A)

OUTPUT – ["teal," "violet," "yellow"]

EXERCISE – Create a list "A" with string data values as "red, jade, teal, violet, yellow" and copy the list "A" to create list "B."

USE YOUR DISCRETION HERE AND WRITE YOUR CODE FIRST

Now, check your code against the correct code below:

A = ["red," "jade," "teal," "violet," "yellow"]
B = A.copy ( )

print (B)

OUTPUT – ["red," "jade," "teal," "violet," "yellow"]

EXERCISE – Create a list "A" with string data values as "red, jade, teal, violet, yellow" and delete the strings "red" and "violet."

Now, check your code against the correct code below:

A = ["red," "jade," "teal," "violet," "yellow"]
del.A [0, 2]
print (A)

OUTPUT – ["jade," "teal," "yellow"]

Python Tuples

In Python, Tuples are collections of data types that cannot be changed but can be arranged in a specific order. Tuples allow for duplicate items and are written within round brackets, as shown in the syntax below.

Tuple = ("string1", "string2", "string3")
print (Tuple)

Similar to the Python List, you can selectively display the desired string from a Tuple by referencing the position of that string inside square bracket in the print command, as shown below.

Tuple = ("string1", "string2", "string3")
print (Tuple [1])

OUTPUT – ("string2")

The concept of **negative indexing** can also be applied to Python Tuple, as shown in the example below:
Tuple = ("string1", "string2", "string3", "string4", "string5")
print (Tuple [-2])

OUTPUT – ("string4")

You will also be able to specify a **range of indexes** by indicating the start and end of a range. The result in values of such command on a Python Tuple would be a new Tuple containing only the indicated items, as shown in the example below:

Tuple = ("string1", "string2", "string3", "string4", "string5", "string6")
print (Tuple [1:5])

OUTPUT – ("string2", "string3", "string4", "string5")

* Remember the first item is at position 0 and the final position of the range, which is the fifth position in this example, is not included.

You can also specify a **range of negative indexes** to Python Tuples, as shown in the example below:

Tuple = ("string1", "string2", "string3", "string4", "string5", "string6")
print (Tuple [-4: -2])

OUTPUT – *("string4", "string5")*

* Remember the last item is at position -1 and the final position of this range, which is the negative fourth position in this example is not included in the Output.

Unlike Python Lists, you cannot directly **change the data value of Python Tuples** after they have been created. However, conversion of a Tuple into a List and then modifying the data value of that List will allow you to subsequently create a Tuple from that updated List. Let's look at the example below:

Tuple1 = ("string1", "string2", "string3", "string4", "string5", "string6")

List1 = list (Tuple1)

List1 [2] = "update this list to create new tuple"

Tuple1 = tuple (List1)

print (Tuple1)

OUTPUT – ("string1", "string2", "update this list to create new tuple," "string4", "string5", "string6")

You can also determine the **length** of a Python Tuple using the "len()" function, as shown in the example below:

Tuple = ("string1", "string2", "string3", "string4", "string5", "string6")

print (len (Tuple))

OUTPUT – 6

You cannot selectively delete items from a Tuple, but you can use the "del" keyword to **delete the Tuple** in its entirety, as shown in the example below:

Tuple = ("string1", "string2", "string3", "string4")

del Tuple

print (Tuple)

OUTPUT – name 'Tuple' is not defined

You can **join multiple Tuples** with the use of the "+" logical operator.

Tuple1 = ("string1", "string2", "string3", "string4")
Tuple2 = (101, 202, 303)

Tuple3 = Tuple1 + Tuple2
print (Tuple3)

OUTPUT – ("string1", "string2", "string3", "string4", 101, 202, 303)

You can also use the "tuple ( )" constructor to create a Tuple, as shown in the example below:

Tuple1 = tuple (("string1", "string2", "string3", "string4"))
print (Tuple1)

EXERCISE – Create a Tuple "X" with string data values as "corn, cilantro, carrot, potato, onion" and display the item at -2 position.

Now, check your code against the correct code below:

```
X = ("corn," "cilantro," "carrot," "potato," "onion")
print (X [-2])
```

OUTPUT – ("potato")

EXERCISE – Create a Tuple "X" with string data values as "corn, cilantro, carrot, potato, onion" and display items ranging from -1 to -3.

Now, check your code against the correct code below:

```
X = ("corn," "cilantro," "carrot," "potato," "onion")
print (X [-3 : -1])
```

OUTPUT – ("carrot," "potato")

EXERCISE – Create a Tuple "X" with string data values as "corn, cilantro, carrot, potato, onion" and change its item from "potato" to "pepper" using List function.

USE YOUR DISCRETION HERE AND WRITE YOUR CODE FIRST*

Now, check your code against the correct code below:

X = ("corn", "cilantro", "carrot", "potato", "onion")
Y = list (X)
Y [4] = "pepper"
X = tuple (Y)

print (X)

OUTPUT – (*"corn", "cilantro", "carrot", "potato",* "pepper")

EXERCISE – Create a Tuple "X" with string data values as "corn, cilantro, carrot" and another Tuple "Y" with numeric data values as (2, 12, 22), then join them together.

USE YOUR DISCRETION HERE AND WRITE YOUR CODE FIRST*

Now, check your code against the correct code below:

X = ("corn," "cilantro," "carrot")
Y = (3, 13, 23)

Z = X + Y
print (Z)

OUTPUT – ("peas," "carrots," "potato," 3, 13, 23)

Python Sets

In Python, Sets are collections of data types that cannot be organized and indexed. Sets do not allow for duplicate items and must be written within curly brackets, as shown in the syntax below.

set = {"string1", "string2", "string3"}
print (set)

Unlike the Python List and Tuple, you cannot selectively display desired items from a Set by referencing the position of that item because the Python Set are not arranged in any order. Therefore, items do not have any indexing. However, the "for" loop can be used on Sets (more on this topic later in this chapter).

Unlike Python Lists, you cannot directly **change the data values of Python Sets** after they have been created. However, you can use the "add ()" method to add a single item to Set and use the "update ( )" method to one or more items to an already existing Set. Let's look at the example below:

set = {"string1", "string2", "string3"}
set. add ("newstring")
print (set)

OUTPUT – {"string1", "string2", "string3", "newstring"}

set = {"string1", "string2", "string3"}
set. update (["newstring1", "newstring2", "newstring3",)
print (set)

OUTPUT – {"string1", "string2", "string3", "newstring1", "newstring2", "newstring3"}

You can also determine the **length** of a Python Set using the "len()" function, as shown in the example below:

set = {"string1", "string2", "string3", "string4", "string5", "string6", "string7"} print (len(set))

OUTPUT – 7

To selectively **delete a specific item from a Set**, the "remove ()" method can be used as shown in the code below:

set = {"string1", "string2", "string3", "string4", "string5"}
set. remove ("string4")
print (set)

OUTPUT – {"string1", "string2", "string3", "string5"}

You can also use the "discard ( )" method to delete specific items from a Set, as shown in the example below:

set = {"string1", "string2", "string3", "string4", "string5"}
set. discard ("string3")
print (set)

OUTPUT – {"string1", "string2", "string4", "string5"}
The "pop ( )" method can be used to selectively delete only the last item of a Set. It must be noted here that since the Python Sets are unordered, any item that the system deems as the last

item will be removed. As a result, the output of this method will be the item that has been removed.

set = {"string1", "string2", "string3", "string4", "string5"}
A = set.pop ( )
print (A)
print (set)

OUTPUT –
String2
{"string1", "string3", "string4", "string5"}

To delete the entire Set, the "del" keyword can be used, as shown below.

set = {"string1", "string2", "string3", "string4", "string5"}
delete set
print (set)

OUTPUT – name 'set' is not defined

To delete all the items from the Set without deleting the variable itself, the "clear ()" method can be used, as shown below.

set = {"string1", "string2", "string3", "string4", "string5"} set.clear ( )

print (set)

OUTPUT – set ( )

You can **join multiple Sets** with the use of the "union ( )" method. The output of this method will be a new Set that contains all items from both the sets. You can also use the "update ( )" method to insert all the items from one set into another without creating a new Set.

Set1 = {"string1", "string2", "string3", "string4", "string5"}

Set2 = {155, 255, 355, 455, 55}

Set3 = Set1.union (Set2)

print (Set3)

OUTPUT – {"string1", 155, "string2", 255, "string3", 355, "string4", 455, "string5", 55}

Set1 = {"string1", "string2", "string3", "string4", "string5"}

Set2 = {155, 255, 355, 455, 55}

Set1.update (Set2)

print (Set1)

OUTPUT – {255, "string1", 155, "string4",55, "string2", 355, "string3", 455, "string5"}

You can also use the "set ( )" constructor to create a Set, as shown in the example below:

Set1 = set (("string1", "string2", "string3", "string4", "string5"))
print (Set1)

OUTPUT – {"string3", "string5", "string2", "string4", "string1"}

EXERCISE – Create a Set "Veg" with string data values as "corn, cilantro, carrot, potato, onion" and add new items "pepper", "celery" and "avocado" to this Set.

USE YOUR DISCRETION HERE AND WRITE YOUR CODE FIRST

Now, check your code against the correct code below:

Veg = {"corn", "cilantro", "carrot", "potato", "onion"}
Veg.update (["pepper", "celery", "avocado"])
print (Veg)

OUTPUT – {"peas", "celery", "onion", "carrots", "broccoli", "avocado", "potato", "pepper"}

EXERCISE – Create a Set "Veg" with string data values as "corn, cilantro, carrot, potato, onion" then delete the last item from this Set.

USE YOUR DISCRETION HERE AND WRITE YOUR CODE FIRST

Now, check your code against the correct code below:

Veg = {"corn", "cilantro", "carrot", "potato", "onion"}
X = Veg.pop ( )
print (X)
print (Veg)

OUTPUT –
broccoli
{"peas", "onion", "carrots", "potato"}

EXERCISE – Create a Set "Veg" with string data values as "corn, cilantro, carrot, potato, onion" and another Set "Veg2" with items as "pepper, eggplant, celery, avocado". Then combine both these Sets to create a third new Set.

USE YOUR DISCRETION HERE AND WRITE YOUR CODE FIRST

Now, check your code against the correct code below:

Veg = {"corn", "cilantro", "carrot", "potato", "onion"}
Veg2 = {"pepper", "eggplant", "celery", "avocado"}

AllVeg = Veg.union (Veg2)   #this Set name may vary as it has not been defined in the exercise

print (AllVeg)

OUTPUT – {"peas", "celery", "onion", "carrots", "eggplant", "broccoli", "avocado", "potato", "pepper"}

Python Dictionary

In Python, Dictionaries are collections of data types that can be changed and indexed but are not arranged in any order. Each item in a Python Dictionary will comprise of a key and its value. Dictionaries do not allow for duplicate items and must be written within curly brackets, as shown in the syntax below.

dict = {

"key01": "value01",

"key02": "value02",

"key03": "value03",

}

print (dict)

You can selectively display desired item value from a Dictionary by referencing to its key inside square brackets in the print command as shown below.

dict = {

"key01": "value01",

"key02": "value02",

"key03": "value03",

}

X = dict ["key02"]

print (X)

OUTPUT – value02

You can also use the "get ( )" method to view the value of a key, as shown in the example below:

```
dict = {
"key01": "value01",
"key02": "value02",
"key03": "value03",
}
```

```
X = dict.get ("key01")
print (X)
```

OUTPUT – value01

There might be instances when you need to **change the value** of a key in a Python Dictionary. This can be accomplished by referring to the key of that item and declaring the new value. Let's look at the example below:

```
dict = {
"key01": "value01",
"key02": "value02",
"key03": "value03",
}
```

```
dict ["key03"] = "NEWvalue"
print (dict)
```

OUTPUT – {"key01": "value01", "key02": "value02", "key03": "NEWvalue"}

You can also determine the **length** of a Python Dictionary using the "len()" function, as shown in the example below:

dict = {
"key01": "value01",
"key02": "value02",
"key03": "value03",
"key4": "value4",
"key5": "value5"
}

print (len (dict))

OUTPUT – 5

Python Dictionary can also be changed by **adding** new index key and assigning a new value to that key, as shown in the example below:

dict = {
"key01": "value01",
"key02": "value02",

"key03": "value03",
}

dict ["NEWkey"] = "NEWvalue"
print (dict)

OUTPUT – {"key01": "value01", "key02": "value02", "key03": "value03", "NEWkey": "NEWvalue"}

There are multiple built-in methods to **delete items** from a Python Dictionary.

- To selectively delete a specific item value, the "pop ()" method can be used with the indicated key name.

  dict = {
  "key01": "value01",
  "key02": "value02",
  "key03": "value03",
  }
  dict.pop ("key01")
  print (dict)

  OUTPUT – { "key02": "value02", "key03": "value03"}

- To selectively delete the item value that was last inserted, the "popitem ()" method can be used with the indicated key name.

dict = {
"key01": "value01",
"key02": "value02",
"key03": "value03",
}
dict.popitem ( )
print (dict)

OUTPUT – { "key01": "value01", "key02": "value02"}

- To selectively delete a specific item value, the "del" keyword can also be used with the indicated key name.

dict = {
"key01": "value01",
"key02": "value02",
"key03": "value03",
}
del dict ("key03")
print (dict)

OUTPUT – { "key01": "value01", "key02": "value02"}

- To delete a Python Dictionary in its entirety, the "del" keyword can also be used as shown in the example below:

dict = {
"key01": "value01",
"key02": "value02",
"key03": "value03",
}
del dict
print (dict)

OUTPUT – name 'dict' is not defined

- To delete all the items from the Dictionary without deleting the Dictionary itself, the "clear ()" method can be used as shown below.

dict = {
"key01": "value01",
"key02": "value02",
"key03": "value03",
}
dict.clear ( )

print (dict)

OUTPUT – { }

There might be instances when you need to **copy** an existing Python Dictionary. This can be accomplished by using the built-in "copy ( )" method or the "dict ( )" method, as shown in the examples below:

dict = {
"key01": "value01",
"key02": "value02",
"key03": "value03",
}
newdict = dict.copy ( )
print (newdict)

OUTPUT – {"key01": "value01", "key02": "value02", "key03": "value03"}

Olddict = {
"key01": "value01",
"key02": "value02",
"key03": "value03",
}

```
newdict = dict (Olddict )
print (newdict)
```

OUTPUT – {"key01": "value01", "key02": "value02", "key03": "value03"}

There is a unique feature that supports multiple Python Dictionaries to be **nested** within another Python Dictionary. You can either create a Dictionary containing child Dictionaries, as shown in the example below:

```
McManiaFamilyDict = {
        "burger1" : {
                "name" : "VegWrap",
                "price" : 3.99
        },
        "burger2" : {
                "name" : "Burger",
                "price" : 6
        },
        "burger3" : {
                "name" : "CheeseBurger",
                "price" : 2.99
        }
}
```

print (McManiaFamilyDict)

OUTPUT - {"burger1" : { "name" : "VegWrap", "price" : 3.99}, "burger2" : {"name" : "Burger", "price" : 6}, "burger3" : {"name" : "CheeseBurger", "price" : 2.99}}

Or you can create a brand new Dictionary that contain other Dictionaries already existing on the system, your code will look like the one below:

```
burgerDict1 : {
        "name" : "VegWrap",
        "price" : 3.99
}

burgerDict2 : {
        "name" : "Burger",
        "price" : 6
}

burgerDict3 : {
        "name" : "CheeseBurger",
        "price" : 2.99
}
```

McManiaFamilyDict = {

     "burgerDict1" : burgerDict1,

     "burgerDict2" : burgerDict2

     "burgerDict3" : burgerDict3

}

print (McManiaFamilyDict)

OUTPUT - {"burger1" : { "name" : "VegWrap", "price" : 3.99}, "burger2" : {"name" : "Burger", "price" : 6}, "burger3" : {"name" : "CheeseBurger", "price" : 2.99}}

Lastly, you can use the "dict ( )" function to create a new Python Dictionary. The key differences when you create items for the Dictionary using this function are: 1. Round brackets are used instead of the curly brackets. 2. Equal to sign is used instead of the semi-colon. Let's look at the example below:

DictwithFunction = dict (key1 = "value1", key2 = "value2", key3 = "value3")

print (DictwithFunction)

OUTPUT – {"key1": "value1", "key2": "value2", "key3": "value3"}

Python supports a large number of built-in methods that can be used on dictionaries. The table below contains all the applicable methods and its usage.

Method	Description
clear ()	Will remove all the elements from the dictionary.
copy ()	Will result in a copy of the dictionary.
from keys ()	Will result in a dictionary with the indicated keys and values.
get ()	Will result in the values of the indicated key.
items ()	Will result in a list containing a tuple for every key-value pair.
keys ()	Will result in a list containing the keys of the dictionary.
pop ()	Will remove the elements with the indicated key.
popitem ()	Will remove the key value pair that was most recently added.
setdefault ()	Will result in the values of the indicated key. In case the key is not found, a new key will be added with the indicated values.
update ()	Will update the dictionary with the indicated key value pairs.
values ()	Will result in a list of all the values in the dictionary.

EXERCISE – Create a Dictionary "CoffeeShop" with items containing keys as "type", "size" and "price" with corresponding values as "cappuccino", "large" and "5.99". Then add a new item with key as "syrup" and value as "caramel".

Now, check your code against the correct code below:

```
CoffeeShop = {
"type" : "cappuccino",
"size" : "large",
"price" : 5.99
}
CoffeeShop ["syrup"] = "caramel"
print (CoffeeShop)
```

OUTPUT – {"type" : "cappuccino", "size" : "large", "price" : 5.99, "syrup" : "caramel"}

EXERCISE – Create a Dictionary "CoffeeShop" with items containing keys as "type", "size" and "price" with corresponding values as "cappuccino", "large" and "5.99". Then use a function to remove the last added item.

USE YOUR DISCRETION HERE AND WRITE YOUR CODE FIRST

Now, check your code against the correct code below:

```
CoffeeShop = {
"type" : "cappuccino",
"size" : "large",
"price" : 5.99
}
CoffeeShop.popitem ( )
print (CoffeeShop)
```

OUTPUT – {"type" : "cappuccino", "size" : "large"}

EXERCISE – Create a Dictionary "CoffeeShop" with a nested dictionary as listed below:

Dictionary Name	Key	Value
Coffee1	name	cappuccino
	size	xlarge
Coffee2	name	espresso
	size	large
Coffee3	name	mocha
	size	small

USE YOUR DISCRETION HERE AND WRITE YOUR CODE FIRST

Now, check your code against the correct code below:

```
CoffeeShop = {
        "coffee1" : {
                "name" : "cappuccino",
                "size" : "xlarge"
        },
        "coffee2" : {
                "name" : "espresso",
                "size" : "large"
        },
        "coffee3" : {
                "name" : "mocha",
                "size" : "small"
        }
}
print (CoffeeShop)
```

OUTPUT - {"coffee1" : { "name" : "cappuccino", "size" : "xlarge"}, "coffee2" : {"name" : "espresso", "size" : "large"}, "coffee3" : {"name" : "mocha", "size" : "small"}}

EXERCISE – Use the "dict ()" function to create a Dictionary "CoffeeShop" with items containing keys as "type", "size" and "price" with corresponding values as "cappuccino", "large" and "5.99".

Now, check your code against the correct code below:

```
CoffeeShop = dict (type = "cappuccino", size = "large", price =
5.99}
print (CoffeeShop)
```

OUTPUT – {"type" : "cappuccino", "size" : "large", "price" : 5.99, "syrup" : "caramel"}

Python Classes and Objects

Python is one of the many object oriented coding languages. Every entity of Python can be considered an object and has its own methods and properties. In Python, Classes are used to construct these objects serving as object blueprints.

A Python Class can be created using the keyword "class" with a predefined property (p) as shown in the syntax below:

class ClassName:

p = 2

A Python Object can then be created from the Python Class created above, as shown in the syntax below:

Object1 = ClassName ( )
print (object1.p)

Built-in Function

In reality, creation of classes and objects is much more complex than the basic syntax provided above. This is where a built-in function to create classes called "__init__()" is used. When the classes are being created, this inherent class function is executed with it. The "__init__()" function is mostly used for assigning values to object properties and other actions that are required for creation of an object. Let's look at the example below to understand this function:

class Vehicle:
        def __init__ (self, name, year)
        self.name = name
        self.name = year

v1 = Vehicle ("BMW", 2018)

print (v1.name)

print (v1.year)

OUTPUT – BMW   2018

Object Methods

There are certain methods that can be created with the Python Objects. These methods can be considered as functions of that object. For example, to create a function that would print a comment regarding ownership of the vehicle and executed on the object v1, the command below will be used:

class Vehicle:

    def __init__ (self, name, year)

    self.name = name

    self.name = year

    def newfunc (ownership):

        print (“I am a proud owner of ” + self.name)

v1 = Vehicle (“BMW”, 2018)

v1.newfunc ()

OUTPUT – I am a proud owner of BMW

Reference Parameter

To refer to the latest instance of a class, the "self" parameter is used. It allows you to access variables that have been derived from a class. This parameter can be named as needed and does not have to be named "self". The important thing to remember here is that the first parameter defined for a class will become the reference parameter for that class, as shown in the example below:

```
class Vehicle:
        def __init__ (refobject, name, year)
        refobject.name = name
        refobject.name = year

        def newfunc (xyz):
                print ("I am a proud owner of " + xyz.name)

v1 = Vehicle ("BMW", 2018)
v1.newfunc ()
```

OUTPUT – I am a proud owner of BMW

There might be instances when you need to **change the properties** of an object. You can easily do so by declaring the new property of the object, as shown in the example below:

class Vehicle:

    def __init__ (refobject, name, year)

    refobject.name = name

    refobject.name = year

    def newfunc (xyz):

        print ("I am a proud owner of " + xyz.name)

v1 = Vehicle ("BMW", 2018)

v1.year = 2019

You can use the "del" keyword to selectively **remove properties of an object**, as shown in the example below:

class Vehicle:

    def __init__ (refobject, name, year)

    refobject.name = name

    refobject.name = year

    def newfunc (xyz):

        print ("I am a proud owner of " + xyz.name)

v1 = Vehicle ("BMW", 2018)

del v1.year

print (v1.age)

OUTPUT – 'Vehicle' object has no 'year' attribute

You can also use the "del" keyword to entirely **delete an object**, as shown in the example below:

class Vehicle:
    def __init__ (refobject, name, year)
    refobject.name = name
    refobject.name = year

    def newfunc (xyz):
        print ("I am a proud owner of " + xyz.name)

v1 = Vehicle ("BMW", 2018)

del v1

OUTPUT – NameError: 'v1' is not defined

The "pass" statement

The definition of a Python Class must contain values or you will receive an error. However, there might be instances when the definition of a class does not have any content. In such case, you can use the "pass" statement to avoid getting an error. Look at the example below:

class Vehicle: # *this class definition is empty*
      pass   # used to avoid any errors

EXERCISE – Create a Class "CoffeeShop" with properties as "type" and "size" with corresponding values as "cappuccino" and "large" respectively.

USE YOUR DISCRETION HERE AND WRITE YOUR CODE FIRST

Now, check your code against the correct code below:

class CoffeeShop:
      def __init__ (refobject, type, size)
      refobject.type = type
      refobject.size = size

c1 = CoffeeShop ("cappuccino", "large")

print (c1.type)

print (c1.size)

OUTPUT – cappuccino   *large*

EXERCISE – Create a Class "CoffeeShop" with properties as "type" and "size" with corresponding values as "cappuccino" and "large" respectively. Create a new function "funct1" that would print "I would like to order a" and execute it on the object.

USE YOUR DISCRETION HERE AND WRITE YOUR CODE FIRST

Now, check your code against the correct code below:

class CoffeeShop:

      def __init__ (refobject, type, size)

      refobject.type = type

      refobject.size = size

      def funct1 (refobject):

      print ("I would like to order a" + refobject.type)

c1 = CoffeeShop ("cappuccino", "large")

c1.funct1 ( )

OUTPUT – I would like to order a cappuccino

Python Operators

In Python, a variety of Operators can be used to perform operations on a Python variable and its values. The different groups of Python operators are provided below:

Arithmetic Operators can be utilized with numerical values to execute basic math calculations.

Name	Operator	Sample
Add	+	P + Q
Subtract	-	P - Q
Multiply	*	P * Q
Divide	/	P / Q
Modulus	%	P % Q
Exponentiation	**	P ** Q
Floor division	//	P // Q

Assignment Operators can be utilized for assignment of values to a variable.

Name	Sample
=	P = 5
+=	P += 3
-=	P -= 3
*=	P *= 3
/=	P /= 3
%=	P %= 3
//=	P //= 3
**=	P **= 3

&=	P &= 3
|=	P |= 3
^=	P ^= 3
>>=	P >>= 3
<<=	P <<= 3

Comparison Operators can be utilized to draw comparison between the values.

Name	Operator	Sample
Equal	==	P == Q
Not equal	!=	P != Q
Greater than	>	P > Q
Less than	<	P < Q
Greater than or equal to	>=	P >= Q
Less than or equal to	<=	P <= Q

Logical Operators can be utilized to generate a combination of conditional statements.

Operator	Usage	Sample
and	Will return "True" if both the statements hold true.	P < 5 and P < 10
or	Will return "True" if one of the statements holds true.	P < 5 or P < 4
not	Will reverse the results and return "False" if the results are true.	not(P < 5 and P < 10)

Identity Operators can be utilized to draw a comparison between two objects to check whether the same object was created more than once using the same memory location.

Operator	Usage	Sample
is	Will return true if the two variables are the same object.	P is Q
is not	Will return true if the two variables are not the same object.	P is not Q

Membership Operators can be utilized to test if select sequence can be found in an object.

Operator	Usage	Sample
in	Will return True if a sequence with a specific value can be found in the object.	P in Q
not in	Will return True if a sequence with a specific value cannot be found in the object.	P not in Q

Bitwise Operators can be utilized to draw a comparison between two numeric values.

Oper ator	Usage	Sample
&	AND	Will set each bit to 1 if the two bits are 1
|	OR	Will set each bit to 1 if one of the two bits is 1
^	XOR	Will set each bit to 1 if only one of the two bits is 1
~	NOT	Will invert all the bits
<<	Zero fill left shift	Shifts left by pushing zero in from the right, making the left most bit to be dropped
>>	Signed right shift	Shifts right by pushing copies of the left most bit in from the left, making the right most bit to be dropped

Chapter 3: Data Visualization and Analysis with Python

Big Data

In 2001, Gartner defined Big data as "Data that contains greater variety arriving in increasing volumes and with ever-higher velocity." This led to the formulation of the "three V's". Big data refers to an avalanche of structured and unstructured data that is endlessly flooding and from a variety of endless data sources. These data sets are too large to be analyzed with traditional analytical tools and technologies but have a plethora of valuable insights hiding underneath.

The "Vs" of Big data

Volume – To be classified as big data the volume of the given data set must be substantially larger than traditional data sets. These data sets are primarily composed of unstructured data with limited structured and semi-structured data. The unstructured data or the data with unknown value can be collected from input sources such as webpages, search history, mobile applications, and social media platforms. The size and customer base of the company is usually proportional to the volume of the data acquired by the company.

Velocity – The speed at which data can be gathered and acted upon the first to the velocity of big data. Companies are increasingly using a combination of on-premise and cloud-based servers to increase the speed of their data collection. The modern-day "Smart Products and Devices" require real-time access to consumer data, in order to be able to provide them a more engaging and enhanced user experience.

Variety – Traditionally a data set would contain majority of structured data with low volume of unstructured and semi-structured data, but the advent of big data has given rise to new unstructured data types such as video, text, audio that require sophisticated tools and technologies to clean and process these data types to extract meaningful insights from them.

Veracity – Another "V" that must be considered for big data analysis is veracity. This refers to the "trustworthiness or the quality" of the data. For example, social media platforms like "Facebook" and "Twitter" with blogs and posts containing a hashtag, acronyms, and all kinds of typing errors can significantly reduce the reliability and accuracy of the data sets.

Value – Data has evolved as a currency of its own with intrinsic value. Just like traditional monetary currencies, the ultimate value of the big data is directly proportional to the insight gathered from it.

"The importance of big data doesn't revolve around how much data you have, but what you do with it. You can take data from any source and analyze it to find answers that enable 1) cost reductions, 2) time reductions, 3) new product development and optimized offerings, and 4) smart decision making."
- SAS

The functioning of big data

There are three important actions required to gain insights from big data:

Integration – The traditional data integration methods such as ETL (Extract, Transform, and Load) are incapable of collating data from a wide variety of unrelated sources and applications that are you at the heart of big data. Advanced tools and technologies are required to analyze big data sets that are exponentially larger than traditional data sets. By integrating big data from these disparate sources, companies are able to analyze and extract valuable insight to grow and maintain their businesses.

Management – Big data management can be defined as "the organization, administration, and governance of large volumes of both structured and unstructured data." Big data requires efficient and cheap storage, which can be accomplished using servers that are on-premises, cloud-based or a combination of both. Companies are able to seamlessly access required data from anywhere across the world and then processing this is a data using required processing engines on an as-needed basis. The goal is to make sure the quality of the data is high-level and can be accessed easily by the required tools and applications. Big data gathered from all kinds of Dale sources including social media platforms, search engine history and call logs. The big data usually contain large sets of unstructured data and the semi-structured data which are stored in a variety of formats. To be able to process and store this complicated data, companies require more powerful and advanced data management software beyond the traditional relational databases and data warehouse platforms.

New platforms are available in the market that is capable of combining big data with the traditional data warehouse systems in a "logical data warehousing architecture." As part of this effort, companies are required to make decisions on what data must be secured for regulatory purposes and compliance, what data must be kept for future analytical purposes, and what data has no future use and can be disposed of. This process is called "data classification," which allows a rapid and efficient analysis of a subset of data to be included in the immediate decision-making process of the company.

Analysis – Once the big data has been collected and is easily accessible, it can be analyzed using advanced analytical tools and technologies. This analysis will provide valuable insight and actionable information. Big data can be explored to make discoveries and develop data models using artificial intelligence and machine learning algorithms.

Big Data Analytics

The terms of big data and big data analytics are often used interchangeably owing to the fact that the inherent purpose of big data is to be analyzed. "Big data analytics" can be defined as a set of qualitative and quantitative methods that can be employed to examine a large amount of unstructured, structured, and semi-structured data to discover data patterns and valuable hidden insights. Big data analytics is the science of analyzing big data to collect metrics, key performance indicators, and Data trends that can be easily lost in the flood of raw data, buy using machine learning algorithms, and automated analytical techniques. The different steps involved in "big data analysis" are:

Gathering Data Requirements – It is important to understand what information or data needs to be gathered to meet the business objective and goals. Data organization is also very critical for efficient and accurate data analysis. Some of the categories in which the data can be organized are gender, age, demographics, location, ethnicity, and income. A decision must also be made on the required data types (qualitative and quantitative) and data values (can be numerical or alphanumerical) to be used for the analysis.

Gathering Data – Raw data can be collected from disparate sources such as social media platforms, computers, cameras, other software applications, company websites, and even third-party data providers. The big data analysis inherently requires large volumes of data, the majority of which is unstructured with a limited amount of structured and semi-structured data.

Data organization and categorization – Depending on the company's infrastructure Data organization could be done on a simple Excel spreadsheet or using and man tools and applications that are capable of processing statistical data. Data must be organized and categorized based on data requirements collected in step one of the big data analysis process.

Cleaning the data – to perform the big data analysis sufficiently and rapidly, it is very important to make sure the data set is void of any redundancy and errors. Only a complete data set fulfilling the Data requirements must have proceeded to the final analysis step. Preprocessing of data is required to make sure the only high-quality data is being analyzed and company resources are being put to good use.

"Big data is high-volume, and high-velocity and/or high-variety information assets that demand cost-effective, innovative forms of information processing that enable enhanced insight, decision making, and process automation."
- Gartner

Analyzing the data – Depending on the insight that is expected to be achieved by the completion of the analysis, any of the following four different types of big data analytics approach can be adopted:

- **Predictive analysis** – This type of analysis is done to generate forecasts and predictions for future plans of the company. By the completion of predictive analysis on the company's big data, the future state of the company can

257

be more precisely predicted and derived from the current state of the company. The business executives are keenly interested in this analysis to make sure the company day-to-day operations are in line with the future vision of the company. For example, to deploy advanced analytical tools and applications in the sales division of a company, the first step is to analyze the leading source of data. Once believes source analysis has been completed, the type and number of communication channels for the sales team must be analyzed. This is followed by the use of machine learning algorithms on customer data to gain insight into how the existing customer base is interacting with the company's products or services. This predictive analysis will conclude with the deployment of artificial intelligence based tools to skyrocket the company's sales.

- **Prescriptive analysis** – Analysis that is carried out by primarily focusing on the business rules and recommendations to generate a selective analytical path as prescribed by the industry standards to boost company performance. The goal of this analysis is to understand the intricacies of various departments of the organization and what measures should be taken by the company to be able to gain insights from its customer data by using a prescribed analytical pathway. This allows the company to embrace domain specificity and conciseness by providing a sharp focus on its existing and future big data analytics process.

- **Descriptive analysis** – All the incoming data received and stored by the company can be analyzed to produce insightful descriptions on the basis of the results obtained. The goal of this analysis is to identify data patterns and current market trends that can be adopted by the company to grow its business. For example, credit card companies often require risk assessment results on all prospective customers to be able to make predictions on the likelihood of the customer failing to make their credit payments and make a decision whether the customer should be approved for the credit or not. This risk assessment it's primarily based on the customer's credit history but also takes into account other influencing factors, including remarks from other financial institutions that the customer had approached for credit, customer income, and financial performance as well as their digital footprint and social media profile.

- **Diagnostic analysis** – As the name suggests, this type of analysis is done to "diagnose" or understand why a certain event unfolded and how that event can be prevented from occurring in the future or replicated if needed. For example, web marketing strategies and campaigns often employ social media platforms to get publicity and increase their goodwill. Not all campaigns are as successful as expected; therefore, learning from failed campaigns is just as important, if not more. Companies can run diagnostic analysis on their campaign by collecting data pertaining to the "social media mentions" of the campaign, number of campaign page views, the average amount of time spent on the campaign page by an individual, number of social media fans and followers of the campaign, online reviews and other related metrics to understand why the campaign failed and how future campaigns can be made more effective.

The big data analysis can be conducted using one or more of the tools listed below:

- Hadoop – Open source data framework.
- Python – Programming language widely used for machine learning.
- SAS – Advanced analytical tool used primarily for big data analysis.
- Tableau – Artificial intelligence based tool used primarily for data visualization.
- SQL – the Programming language used to extract data from relational databases.
- Splunk – Analytical tool used to categorize machine-generated data

- R-programming – the Programming language used primarily for statistical computing.

Big Data Analysis vs. Data Visualization

In the wider data community, data analysis and data visualization are increasingly being used synonymously. Professional data analysts are expected to be able to skillfully represent data using visual tools and formats. On the other hand, new professional job positions called "Data visualization expert" and "data artist" have hit the market. But companies stool need professionals to analyze their data and extract valuable insights from it. As you have learned by now, Data analysis or big data analysis is an "exploratory process" with defined goals and specific questions that need to be answered from a given set of big data. Data visualization pertains to the visual representation of data, using tools as simple as an Excel spreadsheet or as advanced as dashboards created using Tableau. Business executives are always short on time and need to capture a whole lot of details. Therefore, the data analyst is required to use effective visualizations that can significantly lower the amount of time needed to understand the presented data and gather valuable insights from the data.

By developing a variety of visual presentations from the data, an analyst can view the data from different perspectives and identify potential data trends, outliers, gaps, and anything that stands out and warrants further analysis. This process is referred to as "visual analytics." Some of the widely used visual representations of the data are "dashboard reports," "infographics," and "data story." These visual representations are considered as the final deliverable from the big data analysis process but in reality, they frequently serve as a starting point for future political activities. The two completely different activities of data visualization and big data analysis are inherently related and loop into each other by serving as a starting point for as well as the endpoint of the other activity.

Data Analysis Libraries

Data Analysis libraries are sensitive routines and functions that are written in any given language. Software developers require a robust set of libraries to perform complex tasks without needing to rewrite multiple lines of code. Machine learning is largely based on mathematical optimization, probability, and statistics.

Python is the language of choice in the field of data analysis and machine learning credited to consistent development time and flexibility. It is well suited to develop sophisticated models and production engines that can be directly plugged into production systems. One of its greatest assets being an extensive set of libraries that can help researchers who are less equipped with developer knowledge to easily execute data analysis and machine learning.

"Scikit-Learn" has evolved as the gold standard for machine learning and data analysis using Python, offering a wide variety of "supervised" and "unsupervised" machine learning algorithms. It is touted as one of the most user friendly and cleanest machine learning libraries to date. For example, decision trees, clustering, linear and logistics regressions, and K-means. Scikit-learn uses a couple of basic Python libraries: NumPy and SciPy and adds a set of algorithms for data mining tasks, including classification, regression and clustering. It is also capable of implementing tasks like feature selection, transforming data and ensemble methods in only a few lines.

In 2007, David Cournapeau developed the foundational code of Scikit-Learn as part of a "Summer of code" project for "Google." Scikit-learn has become one of Python's most famous open source machine learning libraries since its launch in 2007. But it wasn't until 2010 that Scikit-Learn was released for public use. Scikit-Learn is an open sourced and BSD licensed, data mining and data analysis tool used to develop supervise and unsupervised machine learning algorithms build on Python. Scikit-learn offers machine learning algorithms, including "classification," "regression," "dimensionality reduction," and "clustering." It also offers modules for feature extraction, data processing, and model evaluation.

Designed as an extension to the "SciPy" library, Scikit-Learn is based on "NumPy" and "matplotlib," the most popular Python libraries. NumPy expands Python to support efficient operations on big arrays and multidimensional matrices. Matplotlib offers visualization tools and science computing modules are provided by SciPy. For scholarly studies, Scikit-Learn is popular because it has a well-documented, easy-to-use and flexible API. Developers are able to utilize Scikit-Learn for their experiments with various algorithms by only altering a few lines of the code. Scikit-Learn also provides a variety of training datasets, enabling developers to focus on algorithms instead of data collection and cleaning. Many of the algorithms of Scikit-Learn are quick and scalable to all but huge datasets. Scikit-learn is known for its reliability and automated tests are available for much of the library. Scikit-learn is extremely popular with beginners in machine learning to start implementing simple algorithms.

Prerequisites for application of Scikit-Learn library

The Scikit-Learn library is based on the SciPy (Scientific Python), which needs to be installed before using SciKit-Learn. This stack involves the following:

NumPy (Base n-dimensional array package)

NumPy is the basic package with Python for scientific computing. It includes among other things: "a powerful N-dimensional array object; sophisticated (broadcasting) functions; tools for integrating C/C++ and Fortran code;
Useful linear algebra, Fourier transform, and random number capabilities". NumPy is widely used as an effective multi-dimensional container of generic data in addition to its apparent scientific uses. It is possible to define arbitrary data types. This enables NumPy to integrate with a broad variety of databases seamlessly and quickly. The primary objective of NumPy is the homogeneity of multidimensional array. It consists of an element table (generally numbers), all of which are of the same sort and are indicated by tuples of non-negative integers. The dimensions of NumPy are called "axes," and array class is called "ndarray."

SciPy (Fundamental library for scientific computing)

SciPy is a "collection of mathematical algorithms and convenience functions built on the NumPy extension of Python."

It adds more impact on the interactive Python session, by offering high-level data manipulation and visualization commands and courses for the user. An interactive Python session with SciPy becomes an environment that rivals data processing and system prototyping technologies of systems such as "MATLAB, IDL, Octave, R-Lab, and SciLab."

The additional perk of basing SciPy on Python is that this also makes accessible a strong programming language for use in the development of advanced programs and specific apps. Scientific apps using SciPy benefit from developers around the globe developing extra modules in countless software landscape niches. Everything produced has been made accessible to the Python programmer, from parallel programming to web and database subroutines and classes. These powerful tools are available in addition to the mathematical libraries provided by SciPy.

IPython (Enhanced interactive console)

IPython (Interactive Python) is an interface or command shell for interactive computing using a variety of programming languages. It was originally created for the Python programming language, which supports introspection, rich media, shell syntax, tab completion, and history. Some of the features provided by IPython include: "interactive shells (terminal and

Qt-based); browser-based notebook interface with code, text, math, inline plots and other media support; support for interactive data visualization and use of GUI tool kits; flexible interpreters that can be embedded to load into your own projects; tools for parallel computing."

SymPy (Symbolic mathematics)

Developed by Ondřej Čertík and Aaron Meurer, SymPy is "an open source Python library for symbolic computation." It offers algebra computing capabilities to other apps, either as a stand-alone application or as a library and even as live on the internet applications with "SymPy Live" or "SymPy Gamma." SymPy is easy to install and inspect, owing to the fact that it is completely developed in Python, boasting limited dependencies. SymPy involves characteristics ranging from calculus, algebra, discrete mathematics, and quantum physics to fundamental symbolic arithmetic. The outcome of the computations can be formatted as "LaTeX" code. Combined with a straightforward and extensible code base in a well-known language, the ease of access provided by SymPy makes it a computer algebra system with a comparatively low entry barrier.

Seaborn (data visualization)

Seaborn is derived from the Matplotlib Library and an extremely popular visualization library. It is a high-level library that can generate specific kinds of graphs including heat maps, time series and violin plots.

Matplotlib (Comprehensive 2D/3D plotting)

"Matplotlib" is a 2D plotting library from Python that generates publication quality numbers across a range of hardcopy formats and interactive environments. The "Python script," the "Python" and "IPython shells," the "Jupyter notebook," the web application servers, and four user interface toolkits can be used with matplottib. Matplotlib attempts to further simplify easy tasks and make difficult tasks feasible. With only a few lines of code, you can produce tracks, histograms, power spectra, bar charts, error charts, scatter plots, etc. A MATLAB-like interface is provided for easy plotting of the Pyplot Module, especially when coupled with IPython. As a power user, you can regulate the entire line styles, font's properties and axis properties through an object-oriented interface or through a collection of features similar to the one provided to MATLAB users.

For installation of Matplotlib, either of the pip and conda files listed below are used:

"pip install matplotlib"

"conda install matplotlib"

Creation of basic graphs like linear graphs, bar charts, and histograms can be easily accomplished with the use of Matplotlib. The file below must be imported first:

"import matplotlib.pyplot as plt"

The "iris" and "wine review" dataset used in creation of the plots below using matplotlib can be imported using the pandas "read_csv" method as shown below:

"import pandas as pd
iris = pd.read_csv ('iris.csv', names= ['sepal_length', 'sepal_width', 'petal_length', 'petal_width', 'class'])
print (iris.head ())"

	sepal_length	sepal_width	potal_length	petal width	class
0	5.1	3.5	1.4	0.2	Iris-setosa
1	4.9	3.0	1.4	0.2	Iris-setosa
2	4.7	3.2	1.3	0.2	Iris-setosa
3	4.6	3.1	1.5	0.2	Iris-setosa
4	5.0	3.6	1.4	0.2	Iris-setosa

"wine_reviews = pd.read_csv ('winemag-data-130k-v2.csv', index_col=0)

wine_reviews.head ()"

	country	description	designation	points	price	province	region_1	region_2	taster_name	taster_twitter_handle	title	variety	winery
0	Italy	Aromas include tropical fruit, broom, brimston...	Vulkà Bianco	87	NaN	Sicily & Sardinia	Etna	NaN	Kerin O'Keefe	@kerinokeefe	Nicosia 2013 Vulkà Bianco (Etna)	White Blend	Nicosia
1	Portugal	This is ripe and fruity, a wine that is smooth...	Avidagos	87	15.0	Douro	NaN	NaN	Roger Voss	@vossroger	Quinta dos Avidagos 2011 Avidagos Red (Douro)	Portuguese Red	Quinta dos Avidagos
2	US	Tart and snappy, the flavors of lime flesh and...	NaN	87	14.0	Oregon	Willamette Valley	Willamette Valley	Paul Gregutt	@paulgwine	Rainstorm 2013 Pinot Gris (Willamette Valley)	Pinot Gris	Rainstorm
3	US	Pineapple rind, lemon pith and orange blossom ...	Reserve Late Harvest	87	13.0	Michigan	Lake Michigan Shore	NaN	Alexander Peartree	NaN	St. Julian 2013 Reserve Late Harvest Riesling ...	Riesling	St. Julian
4	US	Much like the regular bottling from 2012, this...	Vintner's Reserve Wild Child Block	87	65.0	Oregon	Willamette Valley	Willamette Valley	Paul Gregutt	@paulgwine	Sweet Cheeks 2012 Vintner's Reserve Wild Child...	Pinot Noir	Sweet Cheeks

Linear Graph

The "plot" method can be used to generate a linear chart in matplotlib. You will able to plot a number of columns in a single graph by looping through those desired columns and plotting them all on the same axis. Below is the sample code for the "iris" data set available on GitHub and the resulting graph for your reference.

"# getting columns to plot
columns = iris.columns.drop (['class'])
 # creation of x data
x_data = range(0, iris.shape [0])
 # creation of figure and axis

```
fig, ax = plt.subplots ()
# plotting each column
for column in columns:
    ax.plot (x_data, iris[column], label=column)
# setting title and legend
ax.set_title ('Iris Dataset')
ax.legend ()"
```

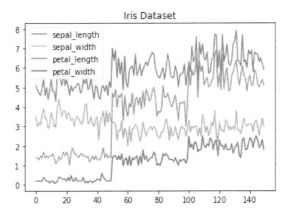

Histogram

The "hist" method can be used to generate a Histogram in matplotlib. The sample code below will allow passing of categorical data such as the points column from the "wine review" dataset to auto calculate the occurrences of each class.

```
"# creation of figure and axis
fig, ax = plt.subplots ()
# plotting histogram
```

```
ax.hist (wine_reviews ['points'])
# setting title and labels
ax.set_title ('Wine Review Scores')
ax.set_xlabel ('Points')
ax.set_ylabel ('Frequency')"
```

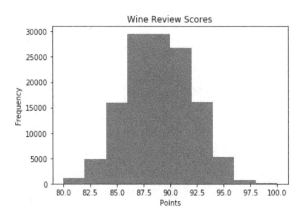

Bar Chart

The "bar" method can be used to generate a bar chart in matplotlib. These charts are not capable of auto calculating the occurrences of each category, so the "value_counts" function from the Pandas library needs to be used. Any set of categorical data lacking a wide variety of categories can be easily plotted using the bar chart. However, any data set containing more than 30 categories of data are too complicated to yield an easy to understand bar chart. The sample code below will allow creation of a bar chart from the "wine review" dataset using the "values_count" function.

"# creation of figure and axis

fig, ax = plt.subplots ()

 # counting the occurrence of each class

data = wine_reviews ['points'].value_counts()

 # getting x and y data

points = data.index

frequency = data.values

 # creation of bar chart

ax.bar (points, frequency)

 # setting title and labels

ax.set_title ('Wine Review Scores')

ax.set_xlabel ('Points')

ax.set_ylabel ('Frequency')"

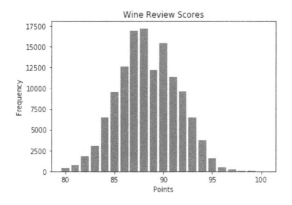

Pandas

Pandas provide highly intuitive and user-friendly high-level data structures. "Pandas" has achieved popularity in the machine learning algorithm developer community, with built-in techniques for data aggregation, grouping, and filtering as well as results of time series analysis. The Pandas library has two primary structures: one-dimensional "Series" and two-dimensional "Data Frames."

Some of the key features provided by "Pandas" are listed below:

- A quick and effective "Data Frame object" with embedded indexing to be used in data manipulation activities.
- Tools to read and write data between internal memory data structures and multiple file formats, such as "CSV" and text, "Microsoft Excel," "SQL databases," and quick "HDF5 format".
- Intelligent data alignment and integrated management of incomplete data by achieving automatic label driven computational alignment and readily manipulating unorganized data into an orderly manner.
- Flexible reconstructing and pivoting of datasets.
- Smart label-based slicing and indexing of big data sets, as well as the creation of data subsets.
- Columns can be added to and removed from data structures to achieve the desired size of the database.

- Aggregation or transformation of data using a sophisticated "Group By" system enabling execution of the "split-apply-combine" technique on the data.

- Highly efficient merge and join functions of the data set.

- "Hierarchical axis indexing" offers a simple way to work in a low dimensional data structure even with high dimensional data.

- Time-series functionalities, including "date range generation and frequency conversion, moving window statistics, moving window linear regressions, date shifting, and lagging." Also the creation of "domain-specific time offsets" and capability of joining time series with no data loss.

- Having most of the underlying code in "Cython" or "C," Pandas boasts high performance and efficiency.

- Python, in combination with Pandas, is being used in a broad range of academic and industrial sectors, including Financial Services, Statistics, Neurobiology, Economics, Marketing and Advertising, Online Data Analytics, among others.

The two types of Data Structures offered by Pandas are: "Pandas DataFrame" and "Pandas Series."

Pandas DataFrame

It is defined as "2-D labeled data structure with columns of a potentially different type". It has a high resemblance to the Excel spreadsheet, as shown in the picture below, with multiple similar features for analysis, modification, and extraction of valuable insights from the data. You can create a "Pandas DataFrame" by entering datasets from "Excel," "CSV," and "MySQL database," among others.

	NAME	AGE	DESIGNATION
1	a	20	VP
2	b	27	CEO
3	c	35	CFO
4	d	55	VP
5	e	18	VP
6	f	21	CEO
7	g	35	MD

For instance, in the picture above assume "Keys" are represented by the name of the columns and "Values" are represented by the list of items in that column, a "Python dictionary" can be used to represent this as shown in the code below:

```
"my_dict = {
    'name' : ["a", "b", "c", "d", "e","f", "g"],
    'age' : [20,27, 35, 55, 18, 21, 35],
    'designation': ["VP", "CEO", "CFO", "VP", "VP", "CEO", "MD"]
}"
```

The "Pandas DataFrame" can be created from this dictionary by using the code below:

"import Pandas as PD
df = pd.DataFrame(my_dict)"

The resulting "DataFrame" is shown in the picture below which resembles the excel spreadsheet:

	age	designation	name
0	20	VP	a
1	27	CEO	b
2	35	CFO	c
3	55	VP	d
4	18	VP	e
5	21	CEO	f
6	35	MD	g

If you would like to define index values for the rows, you will have to add the "index" parameter in the "DataFrame ( )" clause as shown below:

"df = pd.DataFrame(my_dict, index=[1,2,3,4,5,6,7])"

To obtain "string" indexes for the data instead of numeric, use the code below:

"df = pd.DataFrame(

   my_dict,

   index=["First", "Second", "Third", "Fourth", "Fifth", "Sixth",
"Seventh"]

)"

Now, as these index values are uniform, you could execute the code below to utilize the "NumPy arrays" as index values:

"np_arr = np.array([10,20,30,40,50,60,70])
df = pd.DataFrame(my_dict, index=np_arr)"

Similar to "NumPy", the columns of "DataFrame" are also homogeneous. You can use dictionary like syntax or add the column name with "DataFrame", to view the data type of the column, as shown in the code below:

"df['age'].dtype   # Dict Like Syntax
df.age.dtype   # DataFrame.ColumnName
df.name.dtype   # DataFrame.ColumnName"

You can use the code below to selectively view the record or rows available within the "Pandas DataFrame," by using the "head ( )" function for the first five rows and "tail ( )" function for the last five rows. For instance, use the code below to view the first 3 rows of the data:

"df.head(3) # Display first 3 Rows"

Pandas Series

It can be defined as a "one-dimensional labeled array capable of holding data of any type (integer, string, float, python objects)." Simply put, it is like a column in an excel spreadsheet. To generate a "Pandas Series" from an array, a "NumPy" module must be imported and used with "array ()" function, as shown in the code below:

"# import pandas as pd
import pandas as pd"

"# import numpy as np
import numpy as np"

"# simple array
data = np.array (['m','a','c','h','I','n','e'])"

"ser = pd.Series(data)
print(ser)"

Data Visualization with Scatter Plots

A scatter plot can be defined as "a two-dimensional data visualization that uses dots to represent the values obtained for two different variables-one plotted along the x-axis and the other plotted along the y-axis." It is also known as "scatter graph" or "scatter chart." For instance, the "scatter plot" seen in the picture below depicts a fictional set of height and weight measures for children. Each "dot" in the plot is used to represent an individual, with measures of their height along the "x-axis" and weight along the "y-axis."

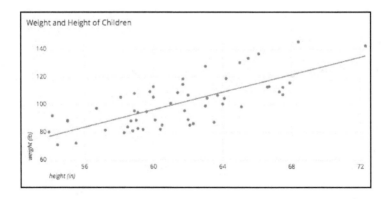

"Scatter plots" are highly useful when you are interested in representing the relationship that exists between two distinct variables. "Scatter plots" are often referred to as "plots of correlation" given the fact that they demonstrate how two distinct variables are related to each other. In the "scatter plot" above, the chart depicts much more than a simple log of the height and weight of children. It also offers a visual of the relationship between the two measures, denoting that as the height increases, the child's weight is also increasing. Now, you can easily conclude that this height and weight relationship isn't ideal, as some taller kids can weigh less than some shorter kids, but the overall trend is fairly satisfactory and it can be observed that there is a direct relationship between the height and weight of children.

It is important to remember that not all relationships can be linear. For instance, the chart in the picture below indicates an "average of daily high temperature" measured over 7 years, demonstrating a familiar parabolic relationship between these variables as the daily high temperature tends to peak during summer.

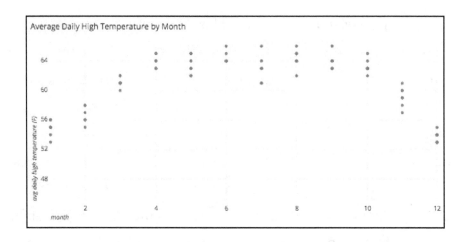

Scatter plots" often contain a trend-line to clarify the relationship between the variable, as shown in the picture below.

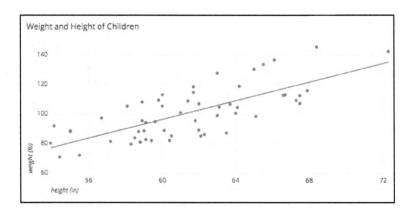

Moreover, the shape, size, and color of the "dot" can be considered and utilized as additional data variables. For instance, the plot below represents the data on the height and weight of the children, but by adding the color of the "dot" to depict the gender of the child, we have acquired a third variable for our analysis.

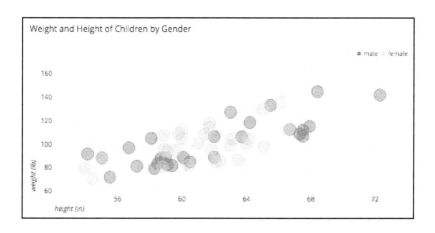

Chapter 4: Machine Learning and Predictive Analysis

Machine Learning

Machine Learning can be defined as a subsidiary of artificial intelligence technology driven by the hypothesis that machines are capable of learning from data by identifying patterns and making decisions with little to no human assistance. The science of machine learning was birthed as a theory that computers have the potential to self-learn specific tasks without needing to be programmed, using the pattern recognition technique. As the machines are exposed to new data, the ability to adapt independently is the iterative aspect of machine learning. They can learn from and train themselves with prior computations to generate credible and reproducible decisions and results. The Machine learning algorithms have been in use for much longer than one would think, but their enhanced capability to analyze "big data" by automatically applying highly complex and sophisticated mathematical calculations rapidly and repeatedly has been developed recently.

Machine learning allows the analysis of large volumes of data and delivers faster and more accurate results. With proper training, this technology can allow organizations to identify profitable opportunities and business risks. Machine learning, in combination with cognitive technologies and artificial intelligence, tends to be even more effective and accurate in processing massive quantities of data. The machine learning algorithms can be categorized into four:

Supervised machine learning algorithms – These algorithms are capable of applying the lessons from the previous runs to new data set using labeled examples to successfully make predictions for the future events. For example, a machine can be programmed with data points labeled as "F" (failed) or "S" (success). The learning algorithm will receive inputs with corresponding correct outputs and run a comparison of its own actual output against the expected or correct, in an attempt to identify errors that can be fixed to make the model more efficient and accurate. With sufficient training, the algorithms are capable of providing 'targets' for any new data input through methods like regression, classification, prediction and ingredient boosting. The analysis starts from a known training data set and the machine learning algorithm then produces an "inferred function" to make future predictions pertaining to the output values. For example, supervised learning algorithm based system are smart enough to anticipate and detect the likelihood of fraudulent credit card transactions being processed.

Unsupervised machine learning algorithms – These algorithms are used in the absence of classified and labeled training data sources. According to SAS, "Unsupervised Learning algorithms are used to study ways in which the system can infer a function to describe a hidden structure from unlabeled data i.e., to explore the data and identify some structure within." Similar to the supervised learning algorithms, these algorithms are able to explore the data and draw inferences from data sets, but cannot figure out the right output. For example, identification of individuals with similar shopping attributes, who can be segmented together and targeted with similar marketing campaigns. These algorithms are widely used to identify data outliers, provide product recommendations, and segment text topics using techniques like "singular value decomposition," "self-organizing maps," and "k-means clustering."

Semi-supervised machine learning algorithms – As the name indicates, these algorithms fall somewhere in between supervised and unsupervised learning and are capable of using labeled as well as unlabeled data as training sources. A typical training set would include the majority of the unlabeled data with a limited volume of the labeled data. The systems running on semi-supervised learning algorithms with methods such as prediction, regression and classification are able to significantly improve their learning accuracy. In situations where the acquired labeled data requires relevant and skilled resources for the machine to be able to train or learn from it, the semi-supervised learning algorithms are best suited. For example, identification of individual faces on a web camera.

Reinforcement Machine learning algorithms – These algorithms are capable of interacting with their environment by producing actions and discovering errors or rewards. The primary characteristics of reinforcement learning are trial and error research method and delayed reward. With the use of these algorithms machines can maximize its performance by automatically determining the ideal behavior within a specific context. The reinforcement signal is simply reward feedback that is required by the machine or software agents to learn which actions yield the fastest and accurate results. These algorithms are frequently used in robotics, gaming and navigation.

Applications of the machine learning technology

Virtual personal assistants

The most popular examples of virtual personal assistants are Siri and Alexa. These systems are capable of providing relevant information using simple voice commands. Machine learning is at the heart of these devices and systems, as they collect and define the information generated with every user interaction and use this information as training data to learn user preferences and provide an enhanced experience.

Predictions while driving

Most of the vehicles today are utilizing GPS navigation services, which collects information such as our current location and driving speed on a centralized server that can be used to generate a map of current traffic. This helps in managing traffic and reducing congestion. With the use of machine learning, system can estimate the regions where and the time of the day when traffic jams occur frequently. Machine learning algorithms allow ride sharing services such as Lyft and Uber, to minimize detours on their routes and provides users an upfront estimate of how much the ride will cost.

Video surveillance

Machines have taken over the monotonous job of monitoring multiple video cameras to ensure security of premises. Machines can track unusual behavior like standing motionless for an extended period of time, sleeping on benches, and stumbling. It can then send an alert to the security personnel who can make the final decision to act on the tip and avoid mishaps. With every iteration of reporting, the surveillance services are improved as the machine learning algorithms learn and improve upon itself.

Social media

Social media platforms such as "Facebook," "Twitter," and "Instagram" are using machine learning algorithms to train the system from user activity and behavior to be able to provide an engaging and enhanced user experience. Some of the examples of the functionalities that are being driven by machine learning algorithms are "People you may know" feature on Facebook (that collects and learns from user activities such as the profiles they visit often, they're own profile and their friends to suggest other Facebook users that they can become friends with) and "Similar Pins" feature on Pinterest (that is driven by computer vision Technology working in tandem with machine learning to identify objects in the images of user's saved "pins" and recommend similar "pins" accordingly).

Email spam and malware filtering

All email clients such as Gmail, Yahoo Mail and Hotmail use machine learning algorithms to ascertain that the spam filter functionality is continuously updated and cannot be penetrated by spammers and malware. Some of the spam filtering techniques that are powered by machine learning are Multi Layered Perceptron and C 4.5 decision tree induction.

Online customer service

Nowadays, most of the e-commerce sites provide users with an option to chat with a customer service representative, which is usually supported by a Chatbot instead of a live executive. These bots use machine learning technology to understand user inquiries and extract information from the website in order to be able to resolve customer issues. With every interaction, Chatbots become smarter and more humanlike.

Refinement of Search Engine Results

Search engines such as "Google," "Yahoo," and "Bing" use machine learning algorithms to provide improved search results pertinent with the user provided keywords. For every search result, the algorithm observes and learns from user activity, such as opening suggested links and the order in which the opened link was displayed as well as time spent on the opened link. This helps the search engine to understand which search results more optimal and any modifications needed to further improve the search results.

Product recommendations

The product recommendation feature has now become the heart and soul of online shopping experience. Machine learning algorithms in combination with artificial intelligence fuel the product recommendation functionality. The system observes and learns from consumer activity and behavior such as past purchases, wish list, recently viewed items, and liked or added to cart items.

Online fraud detection

The financial institutions are relying heavily on machine learning algorithms and artificial intelligence to make cyber space secure by tracking potentially fraudulent monetary transactions online. For example, PayPal is using Machine learning algorithms to prevent money laundering through its platform. They're using a set of artificial intelligence tools in combination with Machine learning algorithms to analyze millions of transactions and distinguish between legitimate and illegitimate transactions between the buyer and the seller. With every transaction, the system learns which transactions are legitimate and which transactions could be potentially fraudulent.

Predictive Analytics

According to SAS, predictive analytics is *"use of data, statistical algorithms, and machine learning techniques to identify the likelihood of future outcomes based on historical data. The goal is to go beyond knowing what has happened to providing a best assessment of what will happen in the future".* Today companies are digging through their past with an eye on the future and this is where artificial intelligence for marketing comes into play, with the application of predictive analytics technology. The success of predictive analytics is directly proportional to the quality of big data collected by the company.

Here are some of the widely used predictive analytics applications for marketing:

Predictive analysis for customer behavior

For the industrial giants like "Amazon," "Apple," and "Netflix," analyzing customer activities and behavior is fundamental to their day to day operations. Smaller businesses are increasingly following in their footsteps to implement predictive analysis in their business model. The development of a customized suite of predictive models for a company is not only capital-intensive but also requires extensive manpower and time. Marketing companies like "AgilOne" offer relatively simple predictive model types with wide applicability across industrial domains.

They have identified three main types of predictive models to analyze customer behavior, which are:

"Propensity models" – These models are used to generate "true or accurate" predictions for customer behavior. Some of the most common propensity models include: "predictive lifetime value," "propensity to buy," "propensity to turn," "propensity to convert," "likelihood of engagement," and "propensity to unsubscribe."

"Cluster models" – These models are used to separate and group customers based on shared attributes such as gender, age, purchase history, and demographics. Some of the most common cluster models include: "product based or category base clustering," "behavioral customs clustering," and "brand based clustering."

"Collaborative filtering" – These models are used to generate products and services and recommendations as well as to recommended advertisements based on prior customer activities and behaviors. Some of the most common collaborative filtering models include: "up sell," "cross sell," and "next sell" recommendations.

The most significant tool used by companies to execute

predictive analytics on customer behavior is "regression analysis," which allows the company to establish correlations between the sale of a particular product and the specific attributes displayed by the purchasing customer. This is achieved by employing "regression coefficients," which are numeric values depicting the degree to which the customer behavior is affected by different variables, and developing a "likelihood score" for future sale of the product.

Qualification and Prioritization of Leads

There are three primary categories employed in business to business or B2B predictive analytics marketing to qualify and prioritize prospective customers or "leads." These categories are:

"**Predictive scoring**" which is used to prioritize prospective customers on the basis of their likelihood to make an actual purchase

"**Identification models**" which are used to identify and acquire new prospective customers on the basis of attributes that are shared with the existing customers of the company.

"**Automated segmentation**," which is used to separate and classify prospective customers on the basis of shared attributes to be targeted with the same personalized marketing strategies and campaigns.

The predictive analytics technology needs a large volume of sales data that serves as a building block and training material to increase the accuracy and efficiency of the predictive models. Small brick-and-mortar companies cannot afford to expand their computing resources. Therefore, are unable to efficiently collect customer behavioral data from their in-store sales. This translates into a competitive edge for larger companies with more advanced computing system, which exacerbates the superfluous growth of larger companies in comparison to small businesses.

Identification of current market trends

Companies can employ "data visualization" tools that allow business executives and managers to gather insights on the current state of the company, simply by visualizing their existing customer behavioral data on a "report or dashboard." These dashboard reports tend to inspire and generate customer behavior driven actions. For example, with the use of data visualization tools, a company can identify the underlying trend of customer demands in specific neighborhoods and accordingly plan to stock their inventory for individual stores. The same information can bring to light the best products and services for the company to be launched on the basis of the current market trends that can suffice the customer demands. The market trend insights can also be applied to increase the efficiency of the company's supply chain management model.

Customer segmentation and targeting

One of the simplest and highly effective way of optimizing a product offer to achieve a rapid turnaround on the company's return on investment is the ability to target "right customers" with appropriate product offers at the "right time." This also happens to be the most common and widely used application of predictive analytics in the world of marketing. According to a research study conducted by the "Aberdeen Group," companies using predictive analytics in their marketing strategies are two times more likely to successfully identify "high value customers." This is where the quality of company's existing data set takes precedence. The highly recommended practice is to use historical consumer behavioral data of all existing customers and analyze it to segment and target customers with similar purchasing attributes with a personalized recommendations and marketing campaigns.

Some of the most common predictive analytics models used, and this application are "affinity analysis," "churn analysis," and "response modeling." Using these applications, companies can gather insight such as "if combining digital and print subscriptions of their product offerings or catalog is a good idea" or "whether their product or service will be more successful if offered as a monthly subscription model or one time purchase fee." One of the leading sales and marketing platform companies is "Salesforce," which offers a cloud based platform that can be used by businesses to generate customer profiles as a product of the data collected from independent sources, including customer relationship management (CRM) applications and other company applications. By selectively and mindfully adding inputted data to this platform, companies can seamlessly track their customer behavior to develop a customer behavioral model overtime that can feed into company's decision-making process in real time and over the long term.

Development of marketing strategies

Another application of predictive analytics and marketing is providing access to a variety of customer related data such as data collected from social media platforms and companies own internal structured data. The customer behavioral model can then be generated by collating all available data and applying "behavioral scoring" on it. All the companies across different industrial sectors are required to adapt to changing or evolving customer behavior through proliferating marketing mediums or channels. For example, companies can use any of the predictive analytics model described above, to precisely predict if their planned marketing campaign would have more success on the social media platforms or on their mobile applications.

Companies are able to employ predictive analytics model to gain an understanding of how their customers are interacting with their products or services based on their feelings or emotions shared on the social media platforms concerning a particular topic. This process is referred to as "sentiment analysis" or "text analysis."

Exploratory analysis of customer data

"Exploratory Data Analysis" or EDA provides a comprehensive view of existing customer data generated pertinent customer data sources such as product prices, current and historical customer surveys, product usage, purchase history, and demographics. It is considered as an approach to look at the data without the use of any statistical model and the data inferences. The term "Exploratory Data Analysis" was coined by John Tukey, in his book released in 1977. Some of the main reasons to use exploratory data analysis are:

- Preliminary selection of the applicable "predictive models."

- Verification of underlying assumptions.
- Make sure the company is asking the right questions to expand its customer base.
- Detect potential data anomalies, redundancies and errors.
- Determination of the relationship between the "explanatory variables."
- Assessment of the direction and size of the relationship between "explanatory variables" and "outcome variables."

The customer data collected in the database form of a rectangular array with individual columns for "subject identifier," "outcome variable" and "explanatory variable." It is rather challenging to look at a spreadsheet filled with numerical values and determine important information from the data and this is where exploratory data analysis techniques are used to selectively display important character is to of the data. There are four types of exploratory data analysis techniques:

1. **"Univariate non-graphical"** - This technique looks at a single variable or data column at a time and displays the results as a statistical summary.
2. **"Multivariate non- graphical"** - This technique looks at two or more variables or data columns at a time and displays the results as a statistical summary.
3. **"Univariate graphical"** - This technique looks at a single variable or data column at a time and displays the results diagrammatically or using pictorial graphs.

4. **"Multivariate graphical"** - This technique looks at two or more variables or data columns at a time and displays the results diagrammatically or using pictorial graphs.

EDA helps in the determination of the best predictive model to address the business problem by generating a low risk and low cost comprehensive report of the data findings and solution recommendations for best suited customer data models. The in-depth exploratory analysis of customer behavior provides exposure to hidden data patterns and market trends that would have been easily lost in the mass of information. Some of the conclusions that can be derived using EDA on customer behavioral data are:

- Identification of customers with the highest number of purchases and the maximum amount of money spent.
- Finding the number of orders generated on a daily, weekly, and monthly basis.
- Identification of the distribution of the unit price for all company products.
- Identify purchase transaction patterns based on demographics and location of the customers.

Personalized marketing with Artificial Intelligence

In a research study sponsored by "Researchscape International," about 75% of the marketing agencies stated that personalize marketing has immensely held their companies and clients in advancing customer relationships, and a whopping 97% stated that they will continue to invest in personalized marketing efforts. This is primarily driven by the fact that companies are able to effectively communicate with their target markets by gathering valuable insights from customer behavioral data using predictive analytics and machine learning algorithms. Typically, personalization starts from an individual customer but can potentially be applied to a segment of customers with shared attributes and achieve "personalization at scale." Artificial intelligence based tools and applications can perform image recognition and voice analysis in combination with customer behavior analysis to provide companies a deeper understanding of customer demands and needs that can be met by delivering precise product recommendations.

Here are some industrial applications of personalized marketing:

Ad targeting

Companies can target advertisements to a specific user or a segment of customers based on their shopping attributes such as recent views of a particular product or category and purchase history. Some of the Ad targeting applications available in the market are:

"ReFUEL4" – The "Ad Analyzer," developed by the marketing company "ReFUEL4", utilizes computer's visual capabilities to predict the performance of the advertisement. If the company's existing ad starts declining in performance, the ad analyzer can help the company to develop a new and better ad. The decline in ad performance typically signals audience fatigue, when people stop paying attention to the ad because it has become too familiar and uninteresting.

"Match2one" – This advertising application can be integrated into the company's e-commerce site and used to I've tracked prospective customers and retain existing customers. The "Match2One" application uses machine learning algorithms to target potential customers that have a higher likelihood of paying consumers. The company claims that it's "engine is trained to generate leads and find new customers using a combination of site visitor behavior and historical data." By analyzing the website visitor data, the application can show targeted ads to the customers hold displayed interest and in particular product.

Personalized messaging

The most important aspect of personalized messaging is contextual marketing. To make sure relevant messages are being sent to the target audience, companies gather customer data, including their behavior, webpage view history, preferred content, social media posts, and demographics, among other variables. Some of the personalized messaging application available in the market are:

"Dynamic yield" – The email solution provided by the company uses customer behavioral data such as order history, email clicks, social media activity, among other features to generate personalized email content for the individual customers. The email solution supplies dynamic email templates that can be easily customized to reflect relevant messages. This application is used across several industrial domains, including travel, E-commerce, gaming industry and social media.

"Yoochoose" – This company offers e-commerce services to online retailers that allows the company to create a "personalized shopping experience" for their consumers, using personalized emails or targeted notifications with newsletters and product recommendations that automatically triggered buy customer behavior. The application is capable of identifying customers who have not made a purchase for some time and trigger a notification to remind them to make a purchase. It can also identify customers who have recently made a purchase and trigger an "after sale, thank you" email. The company offers the "target notifications" functionality along with a product recommendation engine and a "personalized search," all of which are packaged into a "personalization suite."

Product recommendations

The easiest and smartest read for any company to grow their business is to provide accurate product recommendations that are relevant to the needs and demands of the customer. Companies can also reduce the volume and frequency of product returns while increasing their income through new products, repeat purchases and retargeting to entice new potential customers and higher customer loyalty. Some of the product recommendations applications available in the market are:

"Recombee" – This application is based on advance machine learning algorithms that are capable of generating recommendations within "200 millisecond of the customer activity". The company claims that its application can generate over 500 recommendations per second, by employing a combination of "collaborative filtering algorithms" developed for customer behavioral analysis and "content based algorithms" to analyze product titles and descriptions. With every human interaction, the learning algorithms improves upon itself and continues to refine the recommendations with iterative use by the customer. This application is widely used in real estate industry, job boards, classified ad, gaming industry, travel industry and entertainment industry, among others.

"Sentient Aware" – The product recommendation engine offered by "Sentient Aware" analyzes consumer's Visual activity and behavioral interactions to activate the "deep learning algorithms" within the company website. This application utilizes "intent and curation driven algorithms" to identify similar products and the company catalog to generate predictions on customers Preferences and make product recommendations that align with those preferences. The company claims that its application is just as efficient at recommending products for first-time users owing to its capability to generate recommendations without using historical data.

Dynamic websites

A website that can cater to individual site preferences of every customer on-the-fly by dynamically changing its content, which is driven by underlying scripts, is called a "dynamic website." The repetitive tasks including tagging photos and rendering photos, are carried out using artificial intelligence technologies such as "image recognition" and "machine learning." Some of the dynamic website applications available in the market today are:

"Bookmark" – The company "Bookmark" has successfully applied Machine learning technology to web design. The company claims that its "AI Design Assistant" or (AIDA) can custom build company websites pertaining to various website elements, sections and images as well as the overall web design that should feature on the site based on the company's industry specific information. "AIDA" is capable of searching the Internet to gather more information about the client company by running a search on the company name location and type of business. This application collects information on client's customer behavior and activity on social media and analyzes that information to determine the best website elements and design for the company's e-commerce platform.

"LiftIgniter" –The dynamic website recommendation system developed by "LiftIgniter," can be directly integrated with the client's e-commerce platforms online and on mobile applications and is driven by the machine learning algorithm called "true parallel multivariate algorithms infrastructure." This integrated system learns from the customer interactions with the e-commerce platforms and sifts through all of company's online content to display recommended products within 150 milliseconds that the customer might be interested in based on their real time activity on the platform.

Conclusion

Thank you for making it through to the end of *Python for Data Science: A Python Crash Course for Data Science, Data Analysis, Python Machine Learning, and Big Data*, let's hope it was informative and able to provide you with all of the tools you need to achieve your goals whatever they may be.

The next step is to make the best use of your new-found wisdom of Python programming, data science, data analysis, and machine learning that have resulted in the birth of the powerhouse, which is the "Silicon Valley." Businesses across the industrial spectrum with an eye on the future are gradually turning into big technology companies under the shadow of their intended business model. This has been proven with the rise of the "FinTech" industry attributed to the financial institutions and enterprises across the world. This book is filled with real-life examples to help you understand the nitty-gritty of the underlying concepts along with the names and descriptions of multiple tools that you can further explore and selectively implement to make sound choices for the development of a desired machine learning model. Now that you have finished reading this book and mastered the use of Python programming, you are all set to start developing your own Python based machine learning model as well as performing big data analysis using all the open sources readily available and explicitly described in this book. You can position yourself to use your deep knowledge and understanding of all the cutting edge technologies obtained from this book to contribute to the growth of any company and land yourself a new high paying and rewarding job!

Finally, if you found this book useful in any way, a review on Amazon is always appreciated!

www.ingramcontent.com/pod-product-compliance
Lightning Source LLC
LaVergne TN
LVHW051222050326
832903LV00028B/2213